PEOPLES OF THE EARTH

volume 1 Australia and Melanesia (including New Guinea)

volume 2 Africa from the Sahara to the Zambesi

volume 3 Europe (including USSR west of the Urals)

volume 4 Mexico and Central America

volume 5 Islands of the Atlantic (including the Caribbean)

volume 6 Amazonia, Orinoco and pampas

volume 7 Andes

volume 8 The Pacific – Polynesia and Micronesia

volume 9 Southern Africa and Madagascar

volume 10 Indonesia, Philippines and Malaysia

volume 11 South-East Asia

volume 12 The Indian subcontinent (including Ceylon)

volume 13 China (including Tibet), Japan and Korea

volume 14 USSR east of the Urals

volume 15 Western and central Asia

volume 16 The Arctic

volume 17 The Arab World

volume 18 North America

volume 19 Man the craftsman

volume 20 The Future of Mankind. General Index

volume sixteen

Arctic

THE DANBURY PRESS

(Preceding page) A family of Igloolik Eskimo cross the ice with their dog team and sled. Through thousands of years of merciless natural selection the Eskimo learnt how to survive in their harsh homeland and how to use to the fullest extent the sparse resources that the land and sea grudgingly provided for them.

Contents

Supervisory Editor of the Series:
Professor Sir Edward Evans-Pritchard,
Fellow of All Souls, Professor of Social Anthropology,
University of Oxford, 1946-1970,
Chevalier de la Légion d'Honneur

Volume Consultant:
Hugh Brody, MA
Associate of the Scott Polar Research Institute, Cambridge,
Research Officer, Northern Science Research Group, Ottawa

The DANBURY PRESS
a division of GROLIER ENTERPRISES INC.

Publisher
ROBERT B. CLARKE

© 1973 Europa Verlag

Library of Congress Catalog Card No. 72 85614

Printed in Italy by
Arnoldo Mondadori Editore, Verona

8-11   Do different peoples think differently?
Dr Barbara B Lloyd, Lecturer in Social
Psychology, University of Sussex, author of
Perception and Cognition

12-17   Peoples of the Arctic
Farley Mowat, author of *The Siberians* etc (editor)

18-37   Peoples of Alaska
R Kennedy Skipton

38-47   Arctic diggers and explorers
X de Crespigny

Canadian Eskimo
48-61   Netsilik
Professor Asen Balikci, Education Development
Center, Cambridge, Massachusetts, author of
The Netsilik Eskimo etc (editor)

62-83   Igloolik, Caribou and Copper Eskimo
Hugh Brody, MA, Associate of the Scott Polar
Research Institute, Cambridge, Research Officer,
Northern Science Research Group, Ottawa

84-85   Baffin Island Eskimo
David Riches, MA, Lecturer in Social
Anthropology, Queen's University of Belfast

86-97   Polar Eskimo – northern Greenland
Professor Jean Malaurie, Director of the Arctic
Institute of the Sorbonne, author of
The Last Kings of Thule etc

98-103   West Greenland Eskimo
R Kennedy Skipton

104-107   Ammassalamiut – East Greenland
Professor Robert Gessain, Musée de l'Homme,
Paris

108-113   People of Iceland
Magnus Magnussen, author of *Icelandic Stories* etc

114-127   Lapps – Norway, Sweden, Finland
and Russia
Professor Ørnulv Vorren, Tromsø Museum,
co-author of *Lapp Life and Customs* etc

128-137   Chukchi – USSR
Douglas Botting, MA(Oxon), FRGS, author of
One Chilly Siberian Morning and producer of
BBC documentary about Siberia

138-144   Glossary to the peoples
of the Arctic

STAFF CREDITS
Editorial Director **Tom Stacey**

Picture Director **Alexander Low**
Executive Editor **Katherine Ivens**
Art Director **Tom Deas**
Assistant Editor **Elisabeth Meakin**
Project Co-ordinator **Anne Harrison**
Research **Cheryl Moyer**

Specialist Picture Research **Emma Stacey**
Picture Research **Claire Baines/Elly Beintema**
Diana Eggitt/Jeanne Griffiths/Carolyn Keay
Editorial Assistants **Richard Carlisle/Rosamund Ellis**
Mira Bar-Hillel/Susan Rutherford/Pamela Tubby
Editorial Secretary **Caroline Silverman**
Design Assistants **Susan Forster/Richard Kelly**
Cartography **Ron Hayward**
Illustrations **Sandra Archibald, Ron McTrusty**

Production **Roger Multon**
Production Editor **Vanessa Charles**

The publishers gratefully acknowledge help from
the following organizations:
Royal Anthropological Institute, London
Musée de l'Homme, Paris
International African Institute, London
British Museum, London
Royal Geographical Society, London
Scott Polar Research Institute, Cambridge
Royal Asiatic Society, London
Royal Central Asian Society, London
Pitt-Rivers Museum, Oxford
Horniman Museum, London
Institute of Latin American Studies, London

PICTURE CREDITS
Cover: **Guy Gravett, Daily Telegraph, Hugh Simpson, Päl-Nils Nilsson**
(Tiofoto), **Society for Cultural Relations with USSR, Guy Mary-**
Rousselière. Bryan Alexander (Camera Press) 88 tl, 89 t & cl, 90 tl & r,
92-93, 94, 95, 96-97, 114-115, 116, 117, 120-121, 124-125, 126.
Goram Algard 127 tr. **American Museum of Natural History** 35 br,
132-133, 134, 136, 137. **R. Amundsen** (Royal Geog. Soc.) 84 br. **Gôsta**
Andersson (Tiofoto) 119. **Dept. Anthropology & Archeology Cambridge**
Univ. 80-81, 82, 107. **William Bacon** (Rapho, New York) 20 bl, 27 cr,
29 c & bl, 34 cl & tr. **Paul Baich** 42-43. **Barnaby's Picture Library** 89 br.
John Bayliss and Douglas Botting 130. **Sam Bettle** (Rapho, New York)
18-19. **John Bockstoce** 28, (with Arctic Circle Enterprise, 30). **Fred**
Bruemmer 48-49, 58 tl, 66 bl, 68 cl, 76 cr, 77, 78-79, 86-87, 90 bl, 91,
127 cl. **L. T. Burwash** (Royal Geog. Soc.) 84 t, 85. **Ralph Crane** (Time-
Life Inc.) 35 t, 40 tl. **Camera Press** 83. **Daily Telegraph** 50 bl, 51, 59 t &
cl, 69. **J. Feeny** (Photothèque 67 b. **W. Ferchland** 103 bl. **Sven Gillsâter**
(Tiofoto) 32, 33. **Charles Gimpel** 63 tr. **Guy Gravett** (Picture Index) 38.
Cynthia Haas (Woodfin Camp) 101. **Ned Haines** (Rapho, New York)
20 br, 36 tl. From the John Hillelson Agency – **Georg Gerster** 12,
Thomas Sennett 41. **Univ. Washington Library, Seatle** 44, 45, 46, 47. **Erik**
Isakson (Tiofoto) 88 b. **Philip Jones-Griffiths** 22 bl. **Marshall Lockman**
(Black Star, New York) 23 br. **Mats Wibe Lund Jr.** 103 tl & r, 106 tr,
112 cl. **Mansell Collection** 17. **Guy Mary-Rousselière** 2-3, 50 t & br, 52,
53, 58 br, 60-61, 62, 63 br, 64-65, 66 t & br, 67 cl, 70-71, 72, 73, 74 exc.
cl, 76 tr. **John Massey-Stewart** 127 bl. **McAllister of Denver** (Black Star,
New York) 26. **Don McCullen** (Sunday Times) 110 t, 112 tl, 113. **Steve**
McCutcheon (Alaska Pictorial Service) 24-25, 27 tr, 29 tl, 31 tr, 34 tr,
37 t. **B. Mertens** 60 tl, 68 t, 74 cl. **David Moore** (Transworld) 37 br.
Rolf Müller 100 bl. **Nat. Museums of Canada** 14. **Päl-Nils Nilsson**
(Tiofoto) 122-123. **Erhard Otto** 36 tr. **V. Perventsev** (Novosti) 15.
Guiseppe G. Pino 98-99, 100 t. **K. Rasmussen** (Royal Geog. Soc.) 16.
Joe Rychetnik (Black Star, New York) 31 cr. **Hugh Simpson** 104-105,
106 tl & br. **Soc. for Cultural Relations with USSR** 128-129, 131, 135.
Solarfilma 108-109, 110 bl. **Ted Spiegel** (Black Star, New York) 111.
Ted Spiegel (Rapho, New York) 22 t, 23 tr, 40 cl. **Bill Strode** (Black
Star, New York) 54-55, 56, 57, 68 bl. **Van Cleve Photography** 21, 31 br.
Sabine Weiss (Rapho, Paris) 118.
Key: t=top, c=centre, b=bottom, r=right, l=left

Peoples of the Earth, volumes one to twenty

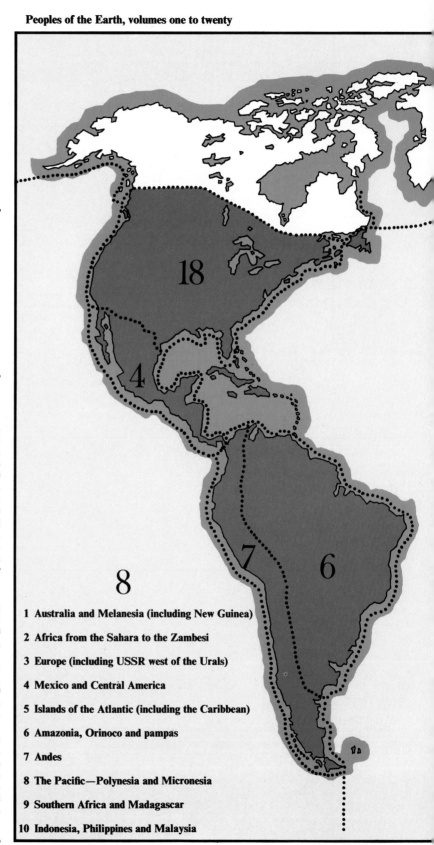

1 **Australia and Melanesia (including New Guinea)**

2 **Africa from the Sahara to the Zambesi**

3 **Europe (including USSR west of the Urals)**

4 **Mexico and Central America**

5 **Islands of the Atlantic (including the Caribbean)**

6 **Amazonia, Orinoco and pampas**

7 **Andes**

8 **The Pacific—Polynesia and Micronesia**

9 **Southern Africa and Madagascar**

10 **Indonesia, Philippines and Malaysia**

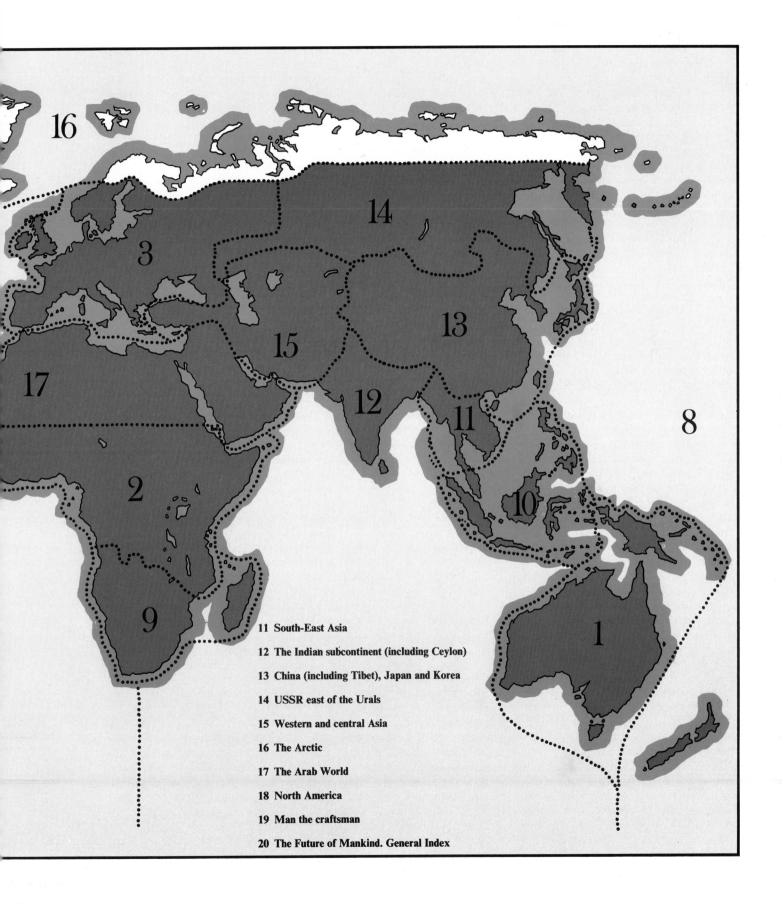

11 South-East Asia

12 The Indian subcontinent (including Ceylon)

13 China (including Tibet), Japan and Korea

14 USSR east of the Urals

15 Western and central Asia

16 The Arctic

17 The Arab World

18 North America

19 Man the craftsman

20 The Future of Mankind. General Index

Do different peoples think differently?

Do people in different cultures think in different ways?' may seem an academic question, trivial or simply uninteresting, but for me it was really brought to life early in my first field study in Kenya. Due to the pressure of paperwork I had, for a week, scarcely ventured outside our house-cum-office in the midst of the Gusii highlands, but my husband had continued our customary visits to the neighboring farm homesteads. Noting my absence, an old woman cheerfully asked whether I had given birth. My husband's negative reply, and his remarks that there had been no visible signs of pregnancy just a few days earlier, did nothing to shake her confidence. She said that European women gave birth differently, that they were unlike the Gusii – whose pregnancies she had watched and in whose childbirths she had assisted.

How can we interpret this explanation of hers? To be an effective midwife she must have been able to recognize the symptoms of pregnancy.

She may of course have been pulling my husband's leg. But it seems equally valid to conclude that when she considered the phenomenon of birth in her own home and in European women she applied a different perceptual theory. The Gusii woman's dual standard reminds me of one early and influential attempt to describe how peoples of diverse cultures think.

Levy-Bruhl, the French sociologist and philosopher, suggested that primitive men think qualitatively differently from western men. He claimed that civilized thought could be characterized in terms of reason, logic and scientific argument and that this contrasted with the emotion-laden, poetic and mythical thought of primitive men. Primitive thought was concrete, based on immediate experience. Western man's thought was abstract. These differences had their source, he held, in varying social milieux and, more particularly, in language. For it is through language that cultures reinforce certain concepts by supplying them with common symbols – words.

Although Levy-Bruhl's analysis of the nature of primitive and civilized thought has not been widely accepted by scholars, the thesis that language and thought are intimately connected has been widely developed. The American linguist Benjamin Whorf, for example, considers – in contrast to the earlier formulations of the primitive mind – that language shapes thought. He also compares the differences between cultures in a deliberately non-evaluative fashion. The linguist's conclusion that human languages are all so complex that it is futile to describe one language as being more developed than another, is also applied to the different thought processes and views of the world which the diverse languages are held to forge. Cultural relativism has been a dominant force in anthropology.

Before rushing to the conclusion that people in different cultures do think differently, and that it is pointless trying to compare them, let us consider what kinds of evidence lead us to this conclusion. We started with what was either a leg-pull or the puzzling logic of a Gusii woman and then went on to some academic arguments which viewed language, a social product, as evidence about how individuals function intellectually.

A result of using social products like language to infer individual processes, like individual thinking, has been confusion in knowing how people who live in different cultures think. The failure to think through both the nature of our question and the kind of evidence we need to answer it led readily to the confusion.

Investigations carried out in the latter part of the 19th century of the basic perceptual processes of different races similarly illustrates this muddled thinking. In the mid-19th century intellectual ferment surrounding Darwin's evolutionary theory there arose speculation about the sharpness of perception of different races.

According to one view the greater skills of the more developed races were demonstrated by their ability to see and differentiate more colors. This argument was supported with the following data: the failure of Homeric Greek to specify colors clearly; and the absence, particularly in the vocabularies of other ancient languages, of a term for blue. Later empirical research demonstrated that individuals could discriminate colors even if their languages lacked the words to describe them.

Our restless, global search for facts may save us from some such pitfalls of Victorian armchair speculation. But it does not guarantee clear thinking about the nature of universal thought processes and the varieties of evidence which can support our theories.

My need to separate individual from cultural questions reflects my own intellectual socialization. As a trained psychologist studying non-western societies I have often thought how different my problems are from those of the anthropologists I have worked with. In the rest of this essay I am going to focus on what kinds of data psychologists collect and what kinds of questions they pose. By this approach I do not mean to imply that this is the only means to understand how men in different societies perceive and know the world in which they live. Indeed, as we shall see shortly, close co-operation between anthropologists and psychologists is probably necessary to produce sound explanations of mental functioning in diverse societies.

One of the earliest scientific investigations of individual perceptual processes in non-western peoples was undertaken as part of an ambitious expedition organized from Cambridge University at the turn of the 20th century. Three psychologists – Rivers, McDougall and Myers – accompanied a team of ethnographers and naturalists to the Torres Straits between Australia and New Guinea. There they investigated the color vision of non-western people. They measured how long individuals took to respond to different signals. They studied their tactile sensibility. And they collected their responses to visual illusions – ambiguous figures deliberately devised to mislead the viewer and lead to faulty perception. The empirical evidence they collected should have laid two prejudices to rest. The 'primitive peoples' they studied showed no greater sensitivity of perception than the Europeans who had been measured on similar tests. And they were no more likely than Europeans to be misled by the illusion figures – although when they were misled the actual patterns of their under- and over-estimations did differ from those of Europeans. Most modern studies have sought to explain these differences by the ways environment affects how people learn to interpret the world. But some current research on responses to illusions relates these to biological factors – to differences in the pigmentation of the retina to visual responses.

The Torres Strait psychologists were guided – in their choice of tasks by which they could study mental functioning – by a psychology that was then still in its infancy. Galton, the gifted gentleman scholar, and Darwin's cousin, had undertaken similar experiments in his attempts to understand the nature of genius. He had identified some interesting differences between the spatial abilities of Bushmen and those of Eskimo. But his efforts to study individual differences in mental ability by using tests of imagery, reaction time and other basic processes of perception were less successful. It was in his research on genius that the idea of measuring the relationship between two variables evolved, and the formal statistic, the correlation coefficient, (later developed with the psychologist Spearman) became a cornerstone of mental testing.

Binet, a psychologist who was working in Paris at about the same time and who was trying to find out how children who would not benefit from ordinary French education could be identified, met with greater success. The collection of tests which he devised predicted school performance. They were used to identify dull, normal and gifted children. The intelligence test, as the collection of tests came to be known, was a ragbag of items. It included assessments of vocabulary of reasoning, number and memory as well as of drawing, picture identification and other complex tasks. After intelligence tests had been used to select American army recruits during World War II they emerged as powerful tools in the practical empirical study of mental functioning. Unlike the earlier attempts to measure individual differences which used simple perceptual responses, the intelligence test, which was composed of complex cognitive tasks, worked. Predictions of success in school that were based on the Binet test were more accurate than those based on teachers' reports or on examinations.

Psychologists subsequently enthusiastically applied those seemingly reliable measures used in intelligence tests to the question of cultural differences in mental ability. In the ensuing 50 years much heat was generated and a little light shed on our problem. It was found that there were large differences in mental ability between one culture and another. Today, when we note that the tests were largely the product of American culture, this does not surprise us. Indeed, when the intelligence tests were used in World War I, men from the southern parts of the United States failed to reach the standards achieved by northerners. Black northerners scored on average higher in the tests than white southerners. Explanations of these differences have been surrounded by controversy. In the efforts that have been made to explain the results of comparative mental testing many factors have been implicated. It suits the purposes of our enquiry to distinguish the more immediate variables which influence test performance from the long-term effects of the socialization of the individual in different environments – although the dividing line between the more immediate variables and the long-term effects of socialization cannot be clear cut. What an individual brings to an experiment obviously affects his behavior in it.

Fear, feelings of strangeness in the test situation, of unfamiliarity with the materials, indeed with the instructions and very language in which the tasks are set are obviously clear sources of difficulty for the individual who participates in the experiment. Less obvious are some basic problems of perception which recent studies embracing more than one culture have revealed. Not only does the culture of the individual impose its own system by which he would interpret ambiguous illusion figures (such as were used in the Torres Strait investigation): there is also evidence that cultural learning also causes variations in rules for determining orientation – and for construing a two-dimensional drawing as a representation of a three-dimensional space.

The psychologist Hudson first began studying the processes by which we infer depth (or a third dimension) from two-dimensional drawings when he was investigating the career aspirations of black South Africans, and realized that they found it difficult to interpret his line drawings. Later systematic research on how the size of objects, super-imposition and linear perspective are seen to indicate depth in simple line drawings has shown that formal education and special training, as well as cultural background, affect the interpretation of depth. In fact some peoples could construct three-dimensional models better than they could copy line drawings. Others again who come from environments where there are no pictures can recognize only the most familiar objects in photographs. The contribution that studies make to our understanding of cultural difference affect mental ability or thinking is that we can see how tasks which seem simple to us, with our cultural background – like identifying common objects from pictures – involve 9 systems of inference which vary from culture to culture. The cognitive demands made on the individual by seemingly simple intelligence tests are in fact very complex and they are not fully understood. We know however, that they reflect the culture in which the tests are constructed and that they give an advantage to those who share the social background of the people who made up the test.

When it was recognized how culture-bound the standard intelligence tests were, efforts were made to devise culture-free instruments of assessing differences in mental ability. Language was seized upon as an obvious source of cultural difference and efforts were made to develop non-verbal testing devices. In the hindsight of comparative studies of orientation and depth we can see the limits of this approach. There has, too, been the evidence from culture-free testing undertaken in the Congo. This evidence shows that scores on these 'unbiased' intelligence scales correlate better with the individual subject's years of schooling – which is of course a culture-bound experience – than with his actual age. We now know that the hope of devising culture-free or even culture-fair means of measuring mental ability is futile. Intelligence testing in non-western settings has nevertheless persisted.

Before we consider alternatives to the concept of intelligence that is used in mental testing we ought to consider how it is or can be applied in developing countries. Because of the practical success of mental testing in selection it has been used for this purpose – understandably, when a year's secondary schooling for a single pupil costs the state more than the average per capita annual income. Whether intelligence and achievement tests should be employed has, however, not only practical but also ideological implications.

The psychologist Irvine made a structural analysis of scores from over 5,000 African school children. In this he showed that his subjects, whose social background differed considerably, displayed similarly organized general reasoning ability and numerical and linguistic factors. He concluded that, unlike a spatial factor – which did vary – the common structures he identified reflected the British origins of education in Kenya, Rhodesia and Zambia. The results were strongly influenced by the particular training the children had received. They did not yield knowledge about their basic intellectual functioning. A report from Uganda further highlights the importance of school experience. It was the quality of the children's primary schooling that best predicts their later secondary school results – even among those students whose achievement test performances at the end of primary education were equal.

We now recognize that intelligence tests measure the skills that are necessary for life in a sophisticated, technological society. It is hardly surprising that the test results of African children who generally come from vastly different cultural backgrounds simply reflect those aspects of western culture which are available to them – the educational system. It is also becoming clear in developing nations that even when selection procedures rely on objective tests and eliminate the bias of personal influence, the children of the westernized élite have a considerable advantage.

Before we look at other attempts to conceptualize intelligence we must in fairness point out that criticism of this approach, the psychometric approach, has in fact come from psychometric researchers. Irvine, for example, has argued that intelligent behavior in other societies may involve skills neglected by current tests, such as interpersonal perceptiveness. A view of intelligence as adaptation to the demands of an environment relates to Piaget's theory of cognitive development.

As a young man Piaget worked in the Paris laboratory of Binet and Simon but was more interested in children's thought processes than in normative responses. His training was both in biology and logic and he views intellectual development as an active adaptation of cognitive structures – which he describes in logico-mathematical terms – to the changing biological and social demands of the environment. He tried with the first cross-cultural tests of his theory to learn whether the different stages in children's thinking appeared at the same ages in children all around the world. He posed the question of how people in different cultures think in terms of a timetable, using European ages as a scale of normal development. The current emphasis in Piagetan theory on the subject's interaction with the environment rather than on his degree of maturity has shifted attention to the inevitability of the sequence described by Piaget.

The first, and universal, major stage of development, according to Piaget's sequence of events, covers the processes of development from birth to two years of age. It has been studied very little as between one culture and another. Considerable energy has been spent, instead, in investigating the hypothesis that non-European, and especially African, infants are born with a precocity of behaviour which persists only for the first couple of years of life. The evidence that this is so is contradictory, however, and the explanations unconvincing. That the first stage of human development, babyhood, is in fact universal is supported by the body of evidence of the development of primates other than man. It is also supported by suggestions that the basic concepts of objects, of time, of space and of causality which are built up during this period may account for similarities in language common to children of different cultures at this age.

Investigations of development in different cultures have focused on the second stage of development when sequences of actions, originally carried out in the real world, become internalized. By and large there is support for the claim that at least in societies with simple agriculture and handicrafts, some aspects of this concrete thinking are universal. But the effects of schooling are less clear. Some researchers find that schooling is necessary for a child to develop concrete operational thought – for concepts such as quantity, for example. Others report that Tiv children in Nigeria, or Chinese children in Hong Kong, can cope adequately with tests that assess concrete operational thought despite their lack of formal education. Results again pose the question whether the particular materials used in these tests to measure concrete operational thinking affect the researcher's diagnosis. Even when the sequence of the child's development described by Piaget has been completed, it is possible for cultural values to alter his further thinking. In a study of the dream concept, the psychologist Kohlberg showed that Formosan adolescents adopted the beliefs of their culture. They believed that dreams are a manifestation of ancestral spirits although children much younger than themselves showed a more mature understanding of dreams. The younger children saw dreams as an internal phenomenon, the product of their own mental processes.

The influence of culture also makes it difficult to assess the final stage in the development of thinking – described by Piaget as the ability to order abstract entities and to employ complex combinatorial rules. Even in western society the development of these formal operations is uneven. In certain fields, where we have advanced training, our thinking may be abstract and complex. In other fields it may not be at a formal level. Clearly from this view of the uneven nature of individual intellectual development the blanket application of the terms 'concrete' and 'abstract' to the thought processes of all individuals in an entire society is inappropriate.

With the working assumption that there is equality of human potential in all societies we have the starting-point of an innovatory research program which uses cultural differences in how individuals perform tasks in order to gain a precise understanding of the nature of particular thought processes. The psychologists Cole and Gay and their colleagues have eschewed overall views of cognitive function, and have examined problem solving, learning, memory and classification with great care and compared the performance of Liberian Kpelle adults and children with Americans of similar ages. Typical of their approach is a series of studies on memory which uses a recall technique of presenting individuals with a series of stimuli to learn and allowing them to reproduce them in any order they wish. By studying the Kpelle noun system the researchers were able to choose stimulus objects in their tests which were known to form clusters in the Kpelle system of concepts. Although they had already found clustered recall in high-school-educated Kpelle

and Americans they went on to study the recall of illiterates. Thorough knowledge of Kpelle culture – as well as skill in experimental techniques – led to the production of equivalent clustered recall when the stimulus objects were embedded in stories and when a cueing technique was employed in testing memory. Cole and Gay argue persuasively for an experimental anthropology which might begin to offer adequate answers to questions of mental functioning in diverse societies.

Clearly psychological investigation of individuals in different societies can yield useful insight into the problem of how different peoples think. We can see more clearly why it is important to be cautious about the nature of the questions that one asks and the kind of data that should be collected. In the heyday of intelligence testing it was assumed that the differences in levels of mental functioning had not only been demonstrated but also understood. But it is now evident that there is considerable confusion about just what the tests were measuring. Although they successfully identified individual differences within a particular society the results could not meaningfully be interpreted to measure cultural adaptation. We can see from our brief survey of Piagetian cross-cultural research that when we view intelligence as adaptation the question of a universal development sequence is still open. One strategy which has helped our understanding of psychological processes to a limited extent is that of using as a starting point cultural differences of approach to specific tasks.

Perhaps the lesson to be learnt is that our initial question 'do people in different cultures think in different ways?' is naive. As we come to understand the complex interrelations of culture and cognition, we ask more precise questions about how different peoples think and what kinds of circumstances are most conducive to the best performance.

Peoples of the Arctic

The Arctic is a mighty land and a strange one. As geological time is reckoned it emerged only yesterday from under the weight of the glaciers and today remains almost as it was when the ponderous mountains of ice finished grinding their way over its face. The Arctic is a new land in every way. To the nations that lay claim to its bleak wastes it is a frontier, a land of wealth undreamt of half a century ago.

Yet in some parts of the Arctic, in Greenland, time seems to have stood still. Five sixths of the land remains buried under the weight of the ice-cap. In the same region nature works with amazing speed. The island of Surtsey, dead brown and bare, was born off the coast of Iceland in 1963 when black and white columns of ash and vapor rose a hundred feet and more out of the sea.

Iceland itself is an island of ice and fire. One eighth of its surface is covered by glacial ice. But the rest of the island resembles a bleak moon-scape, shaped by the activities of 30 volcanoes. The islanders settled on the brief strips of green along the coast and fjords. The Icelandic people are the descendants of Norsemen and Celts. The first settlers were probably Celts from Ireland. Later settlers came from Norway in the 9th and 10th centuries. They brought with them Celtic monks and slaves from the northern British isles.

As the glaciers retreated across Europe and Asia man followed them north until he had eventually settled the whole of the forest and tundra region. These ancient people were small dark men who resembled the mongoloid type. Some of their descendants, the Chukchi (see pages 128–137), live in north-east Siberia today. The northern parts of Europe and west Siberia were then occupied by the Finno-Ugrian people. Their descendants, the Lapps, penetrated far south of the alpine-arctic region of Scandinavia and east to the White Sea. Most of the Lapps today live in Norway. Smaller groups also live in Sweden, Finland and the USSR.

Through the ages, the Arctic has been a gigantic land of refuge for peoples from the south. Many of the Arctic peoples of the Old World have a similar culture, based on reindeer herding, hunting and fishing. Soviet archaeologists believe that reindeer were first domesticated about 4,000 years ago. Through all that time reindeer have supported many of the northern peoples from Norway to the Bering Strait. Some reindeer people stay permanently in the forests. Most are nomads who trek north to the Arctic tundra in summer with their herds and hunt and fish along the coast. Small groups of Lapp and Chukchi have settled permanently along the Arctic coast. They base their lives on fishing and sealing like the

12

From the air it seems as if
no life could survive in
Labrador's desolate waste,
but the Eskimo flourished
in their inhospitable home.

coastal Eskimo who live further east. Across the Bering Strait much of the Arctic coastline from Alaska across Canada to Greenland has been inhabited by Eskimo.

Racially the Eskimo are allied to the Asiatic fathers of the Chukchi. Thousands of years before Christ, possibly about 6,000 years ago, the people who were then living in the eastern plains of Siberia were driven north and east by warlike hordes from Asia. The Siberian plains dwellers were reindeer hunters who knew nothing of war. Eventually they crossed the narrow Bering Strait to Alaska. Some of them settled on the Aleutian Islands. They spread westward from one island to another but did not dare to cross the broad gap to the Komandorskiye Islands. The Aleutian islanders soon became isolated from the rest of their people and developed their own culture. Unlike the other Arctic peoples they did not have to adapt to an environment of snow and ice. The sea around the islands does not freeze. The climate is cool, rainy and foggy with little snow.

The rest of the fugitives from Siberia probably found Alaska occupied by the forebears of the Indians. The coast may have already been settled by earlier immigrants from the Siberian coast who had developed a sea culture and spread eastward. The Siberian plains people were forced to move inland through the tundra plains until they found unoccupied land. The Eskimo ethnologist, Knud Rasmussen has called these people proto-Eskimo. From them, the whole Eskimo race probably developed, although with other admixtures of neolithic people, some of whom may perhaps have originally come from Europe via the northern isles. Through the thousands of years of their occupation of the top of the world the Eskimo were subject to the most merciless selection of nature, They adapted in physique and spirit, technique and knowledge and became the masters of their Arctic world.

The early proto-Eskimo people worked through the Brooks Mountain barrens in northern Alaska until they reached the true flat Barrens near Great Bear Lake. These rolling plains would have been like home to the wanderers. The tundra to the north and east of Great Bear is very similar to the northern treeless steppes of Siberia. The animals too would have been familiar. The white fox, the lemming, the wolf and the caribou as well as many other animals are identical in Siberia and northern Canada. An immigrant race who had lived on reindeer would find no difficulty in building a life around the caribou, which are first cousins to the reindeer.

After the people from Siberia settled in the central Arctic plains two things began to happen. The caribou made their annual migrations north each spring to the Arctic coast. Over a long period, beginning perhaps 5,000 years ago, some of the settlers from the Arctic plains reached the coast in seasonal pursuit of migrating deer. These people eventually developed a mixed sea and caribou culture which spread west and east across the high Arctic from Alaska to Greenland. Eventually it evolved into a complete sea culture based on the hunting of seal, walrus and whales.

Very much later, about 300 years ago, a new factor disturbed the life of the remaining tundra Eskimo who had stayed on in the interior plains. They were subjected to pressures from people living to the south. This time the pressure came from the Indians. Armed with guns obtained from European traders, the Indians of the prairies just south of the Canadian forests began to move north. The Cree Indians were pushed out of the plains and forced high up into the forests. They pressed against the southern flanks of a primitive group of Chipewyans, the Athapascan Indians. The Athapascans moved north out of the forests and adapted themselves to the ways of the migratory deer.

It was inevitable that they should encroach on the land of the proto-Eskimo and also inevitable that blood would be shed. Bloody tales of those times remain in the folklore of the inland Eskimo. A war of attrition and survival of ancient origins continued almost to the end of the 19th century with undiminished ferocity. It was a one-sided war for the Eskimo were not warriors. They were forced toward the Arctic wastes by the Indians, as had happened in Siberia. Folklore tells of their great trek in search of new lands to settle. Some of the fugitives fled north toward the coast. These people settled on the Arctic coast around Coronation Gulf and developed a new culture adapted to the demands of the sea. The rest went east into the depths of the Barrens.

So the culture of the Eskimo developed in a variety of ways brought about by change, migration and the inter-mixing of local groups. As time passed their descendants who had learned to combat the sea spread westward to the Pacific coast of Alaska and eastward as far as Greenland. Today the northernmost living human beings are the high-Arctic Polar Eskimo. They settled in what is now the Thule district in Greenland. The East Greenland Eskimo live around Angmagssalik and Scoresby Sound. The West Greenlanders live along the entire low-Arctic west coast from Melville Bay to Cape Farewell.

But the men who had lived on the plains since the dawn of their history steadfastly remained on the plains. The last group of proto-Eskimo finally settled on the great plain inland from Hudson Bay around Dubwant, Yathkyed and Angikuni Lakes in Keewatin Territory

The first Europeans reached Hudson Bay early in the 17th century. By that time the inland Eskimo had long been settled on the inland tundra. The whole of the tundra west as far as the Back River and south from the timberline to the fringe of the Arctic coast were in the hands of a great multitude of inland Eskimo who depended for their whole livelihood upon the caribou.

They were a fortunate people. Through the next two centuries, while the white men changed and mutilated 13

Peoples of the Arctic

Eskimo are descended from a migrant Asian people who crossed the Bering Strait to Alaska thousands of years ago and settled in the Arctic.

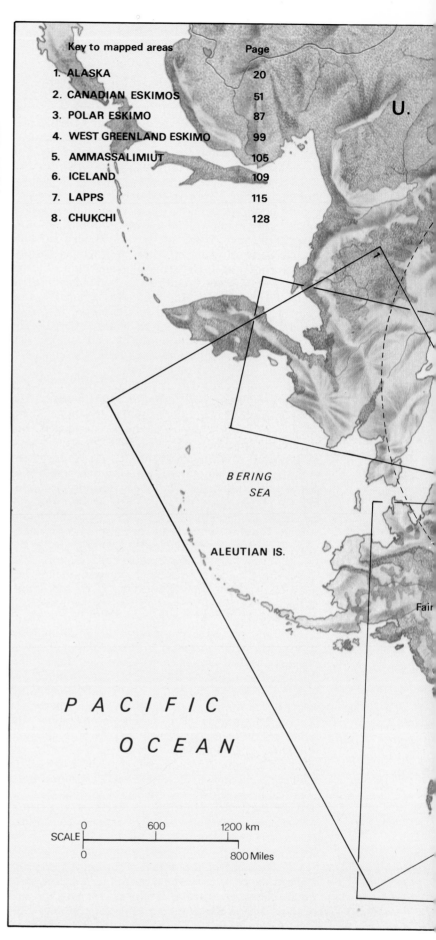

Key to mapped areas	Page
1. ALASKA	20
2. CANADIAN ESKIMOS	51
3. POLAR ESKIMO	87
4. WEST GREENLAND ESKIMO	99
5. AMMASSALIMIUT	105
6. ICELAND	109
7. LAPPS	115
8. CHUKCHI	128

U.

BERING
SEA

ALEUTIAN IS.

PACIFIC

OCEAN

Fair

SCALE 0   600   1200 km
      0   800 Miles

the lives of many coast Eskimo and Indians, the inland people remained remote. Yet indirectly, the white men brought a change in their lives. Ever since their first ancient contacts, the Eskimo and the Chipewyan Indians had remained aloof from one another. Neither were a warlike people and so, except for isolated incidents, they had left a broad band of uninhabited country between them. Then the Chipewyan began to barter for guns. Before the end of the 18th century they had begun to force the Eskimo out of the land which had been theirs for centuries.

But the Indians held the northern land for only a few decades. Smallpox came burning up from the south and swept north, decimating entire Indian tribes. The isolated inland Eskimo were spared the plague and slowly edged southwards again until they reached the limits of the forests. Through all this time they had no contact with white men and very little with the coast Eskimo who were now trading with the Hudson's Bay Company at Eskimo Point and Marble Island.

The inland Eskimo were a great people in those days. As many as 2,000 lived in their camps. They called

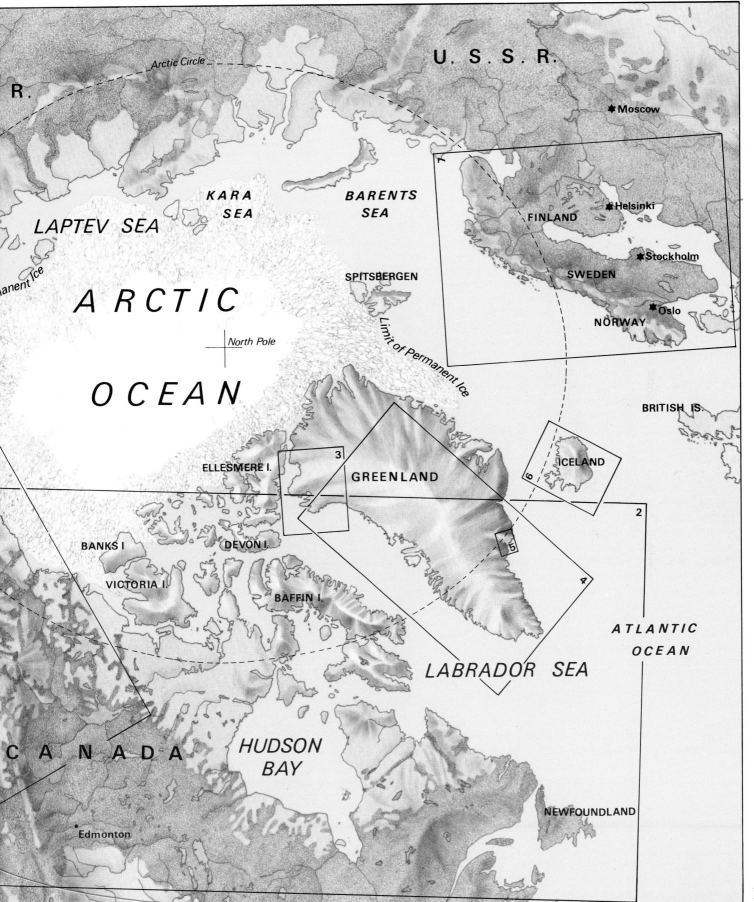

R.

U. S. S. R.

★ Moscow

KARA
SEA

BARENTS
SEA

LAPTEV SEA

Arctic Circle

FINLAND

★ Helsinki

1

SPITSBERGEN

★ Stockholm

SWEDEN

manent Ice

ARCTIC

North Pole

Limit of Permanent Ice

NORWAY

★ Oslo

OCEAN

BRITISH IS.

ELLESMERE I.

3

GREENLAND

ICELAND

6

2

BANKS I.

DEVON I.

5

VICTORIA I.

BAFFIN I.

4

ATLANTIC
OCEAN

LABRADOR SEA

C A N A D A

HUDSON
BAY

NEWFOUNDLAND

• Edmonton

themselves Ihalmiut. It is a name with a proud ring, for it means 'The Other People' – those who are set apart from and superior to all others. They were indeed set apart. It was not until 1867 that a missionary, the first of the strangers who had already usurped a continent, came into their land. As a result of this visit, small and courageous groups of the best hunters began to trade with the missionary and the Hudson's Bay Company post at Reindeer Lake.

Immediately after the turn of the century the inland people were among the most numerous and cohesive group of Eskimo. They were also among the most secure and the most vital. Unlike the majority of coastal and sea-culture Eskimo, they were not nomads. They were a settled people of long established residence in their camps along the rivers and beside the lakes. The caribou, on which their entire way of life was based, came to them twice and often four times a year, in mighty herds that stretched as far as a man's eye could encompass. The inland Eskimo did not follow the coastal Eskimo into virtual servitude to trading post and mission. They were a rich people, as richness is measured in their world, for they seldom knew hunger or cold. The deer and musk oxen were abundant. The Ihalmiut had no need to suffer through long bitter winter days upon the ice seeking seals; nor on the frozen lakes jigging stubbornly for fish. Instead of being a time of hardship and dread, as it was for many Eskimo groups their winter was a time for feasting, for visiting, for songs and stories. They had time to dream and work with words and thoughts – while their cousins on the hard sea coasts had little time for anything except the eternal struggle to survive.

Yet the white man brought tragedy to these Eskimo. In 1947 a message was sent out from the trading post at Reindeer Lake to say that some of the inland people, 46 of them, were in danger of starving to death. The inland Eskimo had been defeated.

Traders and furtrappers who came to the Arctic regarded the land's untapped wealth as miners think of a rich lode hidden deep in the mountains. The Hudson's Bay Company had, until the 19th century, legally possessed almost the whole of the Canadian Arctic. The Company's profits in the north were derived almost solely from the fur trade. Most of the trapping was done for them by the Eskimo and northern Indians. The traders persuaded the northern peoples to believe that the pursuit of fox pelts was more desirable than the pursuit of meat. It did not take long for the Indians and Eskimo to realize that trading fox pelts for guns, ammunition and flour was easier than hunting caribou or seals with spears. And so, in a few decades they learned to neglect the caches of meat they used to make every autumn. But when trading ceased to fetch high prices, when the price of furs fell in the markets of Europe and America, the traders withdrew. The new way of life that had been taught to the people became

their death. They had forgotten how to make the traditional weapons of their fathers. Without ammunition from the traders, their guns were useless. The other evil that the white man brought the Eskimo was disease. Very many of Indians and Eskimo were wiped out by influenza, diphtheria, polio, tuberculosis.

The animals of the Arctic too became victims. The caribou were slaughtered in tens of thousands. The caribou were destroyed by a combination of rifles and unlimited ammunition and by the wanton and gigantic wastage of the forests to the south by fire. The lichens and mosses which alone enabled the herds to survive upon the winter range were destroyed with the forests. Biologists have shown that it takes up to 100 years for the spruce-lichen forests to renew themselves. The fires were set alight, for the most part, by prospectors to expose the naked rocks, or by settlers anxious to clear the land. The fate of the caribou has been the fate of other animals of the Canadian Arctic. The whalers have long since destroyed the great mammals which once came into Hudson Bay and into all the narrow waters at the top of the continent. The walrus which were once the most important of the sea beasts to the coast Eskimo

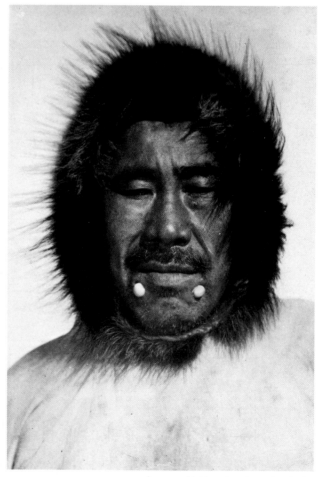

Now only a few old people among the Copper Eskimo wear bone labrets, once thought to enhance the wearer's appeal to the opposite sex.

have been seriously reduced.

It was not until 1958 that the true situation among the Canadian Eskimo became known. One out of every eight surviving Eskimo had a history of tuberculosis. The life expectancy of an Eskimo was slightly more than 24 years. The infant mortality rate was more than 260 deaths for every 1,000 births.

In the late 1950s the white man's governments had begun to see the Arctic in a new light. Most Canadians and Americans had traditionally considered the Arctic to be a useless and sterile waste. But it was becoming increasingly obvious that the Arctic held a good many economic opportunities. The realization of the Arctic's vast mineral resources, particularly oil, prompted what was to be another gold rush. The north had also become an area of strategic importance and military activity developed rapidly. Eskimo were employed, experimentally, at a nickel mine. Within two years Eskimo who had never previously experienced any society more complex than that of seal hunters and fox trappers, had overleapt the barriers of time and had almost taken over the operation of the mine. By 1965 the hunting and trapping base had virtually disappeared. Almost every Eskimo family in Canada now lives in government-staffed villages along the coast. Unhappily, they have not really been given a chance to find new lives in our modern world of technology, and today the vast majority of them, unable to return to the old days, and without any chance to acquire new ways, live on relief or Government assistance. The changes for the Alaskan Eskimo were less dramatically sudden. The incorporation of wage and welfare economy and involvement with a white frontier society started two generations ago, but even there the native people have been excluded from equal participation in our world.

Russia realized the importance of the northern regions long before Canada and America. Gold, diamonds, tin and other minerals are being mined in Siberia. In the 1950s when the USSR began to move north in earnest it was realized that the north already possessed the means of feeding the rapidly growing population. Virtually the only food that can be produced in the north is reindeer. Reindeer herding now provides a solid economic base for about 12,000 Chukchi and Eskimo. Reindeer breeding has become one of the most profitable of all types of animal husbandry. The animals are hardy and self-sufficient. They need no hay or planted crops and no buildings to shelter them.

Norway, Sweden and Finland between them have a base herd of a million animals. It was once believed that northern Canada and Alaska could together carry a herd of 5 million animals, and provide an economic *raison d'être* for all the northern natives Attempts were made to start herding. Some Lapps were brought to Canada to teach the Eskimo herding techniques. The scheme has however, remained nothing more

than an experiment, limited to a tiny handful of Eskimo and beset with economic difficulties.

The Greenland Eskimo have prospered more than any others. In 1952 the Danish government announced the penultimate step in the development of an Eskimo nation in Greenland. Eskimo took over their own internal government. As far back as 1860 the Danes had eliminated illiteracy in Greenland, whereas only a few score of Canadian Eskimo were literate in the 1950s. In the early days of Danish interest in Greenland, laws had been passed to curb purely selfish commercial exploitation by white men. The only trading posts allowed were run by the government. Denmark had begun to give a measure of independent self-government to the Greenland Eskimo, as early as 1900. Today the descendants of men who once speared seals, teach in schools and take an important part in industry. The Eskimo run a lucrative fishing industry. They help operate the intricate scientific apparatus of weather stations. In effect the Greenlanders now own their own economy, though it is supervised by Danish administrators. As in the rest of the Arctic, much of Greenland is too harsh for European comfort. But the Eskimo are a part of their land. They possess the physical and mental heritages of their race who long since learned to live and prosper in that inhospitable region.

The time has come when the nations who rule the Arctic are beginning to exploit fully of the world's sole remaining frontier. It is not a casual exploitation of surface resources. It is a long-term attack. One of the last remaining undeveloped regions of the earth is being rapidly reshaped.

Eskimo are scattered across the Arctic from Siberia to Greenland, yet everywhere their language has remained the same.

Peoples of Alaska

Eskimo vitality is on show at winter festivals like this one at Barrow, northern tip of Alaska, where a man springs on a sealskin trampoline.

Alaska, the most northerly state of America, is a land lying between two worlds. There is wilderness in Alaska, from frozen Arctic wastelands to untroubled zones of forest; from the verdant south-east, to the buffeted chain of the Aleutian islands. Sometimes, in the depths of winter, it seems as though Alaska is half a million square miles of silence. In places the temperature falls to 50° below freezing and for days the darkness is barely broken by the sun. In Alaska, the wildlife outnumbers the men. Virgin spruce forests, marshy muskeg country and mountain tundra are only thinly populated by moose and caribou, dall sheep and bears.

Few people live in Alaska, a land half the size of western Europe. All of the 285,000 Alaskans could be easily lost in a city the size of San Francisco. As it is half of those Alaskans live in Anchorage, the main town, where they lead centrally-heated, modern lives, hardly different from their counterparts in towns and cities of the southern forty-nine states of America. The rest of the Alaskans are scattered in other towns, like Sitka and Juneau (the capital), or Barrow more than 300 miles above the Arctic circle, or Nome in the west – small towns with streets that recall another century and other buildings, which have grown in the last few years.

Only some 54,000 Alaskans are Eskimo, Aleut or Indian, indigenous to this land. Others have come from the USA, perhaps as long ago as the years of the gold rush, and their children have remained. Some are adventurers, escaping overcrowded cities; some are trappers or hunters, guides, charter pilots, even gold-panners. And for those who do not live in the towns, there is elbow room as far as the eye can see. Alaska seems to breed superlatives. It is the largest state of the USA with the smallest population; it has the highest mountain, the coldest winter and a summer where, in places, the sun never sets.

Like America's west 100 years ago, Alaska is a frontier to which men are drawn with the intention of changing at least some part of it. The wilderness conceals wealth like gold and oil; the seas surrounding the western coasts are fertile fishing grounds; the forests are themselves a currency. The gold rush to the Yukon in the 1890s brought thousands of prospectors and took Alaska to the ears of America; but oil, the black gold, has opened up Alaska to the eyes of the world. Now the flames of gas burn-offs above the oil wells south of Anchorage burn through the hours of day and night. This is the other world of Alaska.

The history of modern Alaska began only in the early part of the 18th century when Peter the Great, Tsar of Russia, instructed a sea captain named Vitus Bering to explore the far eastern coasts of Siberia. The Tsar was interested to know if the continents of Russia and America were joined in the far north. Bering's interest in this assignment turned lukewarm when he had sailed far enough to satisfy himself that there was a sea between 19

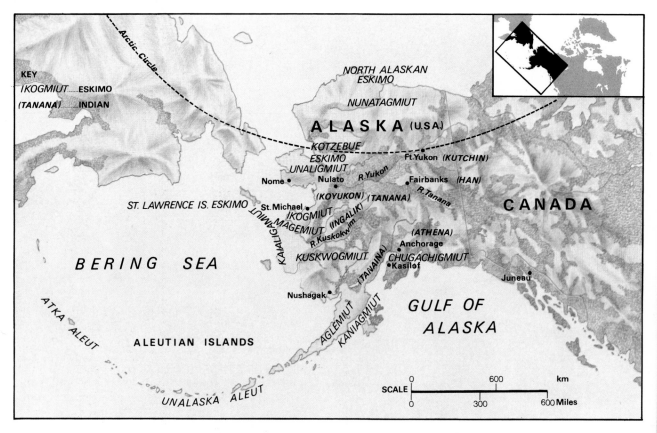

Many Eskimo now wear glasses because of a gradual snow blindness — the result of a lifetime's squinting against reflected sunlight.

The Northern Lights, *aurora borealis*, appearing at Fairbanks in a temperature of −40°, are shaped by luminous electrical particles.

Winter seal hunters build
driftwood shacks along the
coast. Sometimes they live
there permanently with their
families and everyone fishes.

Peoples of Alaska

The overall radiation count on an Eskimo is tested at Kotzebue. Alaskan people have suffered in the past from the ill effects of nuclear tests.

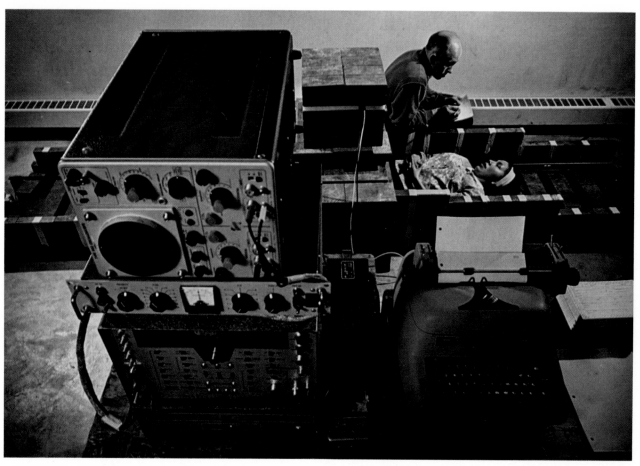

the two continents. On his return he announced that there was no good reason for any further exploration. A series of incidents had prevented him from discovering much unknown territory to the east. But Bering's voyage had generated much interest and several geographers discredited his reports. Plans were then made to launch another expedition. This second voyage, though fraught with disaster, decided the Russians that the great land to the east was worth further exploration and colonization. Bering did not return, but the survivors brought back a good cargo of furs and sea-otter skins. The land in the east was named Russian America and Russians began to settle there.

During the following century the Russians sailed, explored, traded and colonized as far as California. But other nations were already showing interest in Alaska, looking for toe-holds for settlements, or a chance to extract some wealth from the land. At times, however, all was not peaceful. At the place which is now the town of Sitka Bering's second in command had dropped anchor among the islands. He sent a boatload of sailors ashore, but they failed to return. Three days later he dispatched a second boat, but none of that crew returned. In vain the ship waited for three weeks before

22

Polling day in Anchorage, the crowded modern city where half the Alaskans live. Alaska has a population of less than one person per square mile.

The congregation at this chapel in Anaktuvuk pass is almost all Eskimo. They are regular churchgoers who have Christianized their rituals.

raising anchor and setting out to sea. Nothing was ever heard of the fate of those crew-members who had made landfall, except in an Indian myth. According to this a chieftain had dressed himself in bearskins and lured them to their deaths. This was the white man's first encounter with the Tlingit tribe of Indians. Blood was to be shed many times again.

Russian fur traders set out from Siberia and discovered the Aleutian islands whose desolate mountains rose from the sea, a craggy buffer between the north Pacific and the Bering sea. Here was a land of rocks and solidified lava whose mountains were furrowed, shaped like cones, and covered with bird droppings from the sea to the edge of their craters. The Russians felt 'thundering earthquakes', watched 'a rain of fire from volcanic eruptions'. In winter the wind was bitter. In summer rain blanketed the hills. And here they found the Aleut, a group of Eskimo who called themselves the 'Brothers of the Sea Otter'.

The Aleut were a short people, but sturdy. They seemed to have a sparse growth of hair and the color of their skin was like that of the people of northern Japan. The sea was their livelihood and in their skin-covered *bidarka* they paddled through astonishing seas carrying bows and arrows and simple fishing tackle. They were a peaceful people and their numbers soon began to dwindle. Today less than 4,000 of them remain.

The Russians pushed on east and found that the islands became larger, where hills covered with grass and lava rose from the sea into foothills farther inland, and where glaciers bridged the narrow fjords. This was the vast territory of the Tlingit Indians who had already met the white men. They were a proud tribe who lived in a highly organized society. They built large log cabins in which many families lived together. They paddled great distances in their longboats, plundering and taking slaves from other tribes. Each boat held as many as 20 warriors wearing helmets, body armor and carrying shields. Today there are only a few thousand of this tribe still living. The manager of the Russian-American trading company built a wooden fort overlooking Sitka harbor in 1802. He ruled over the Aleut ruthlessly; he fought against the Tlingit Indians. And at that time Sitka was a glamorous and gay town, with adventurers, trappers and traders congregating there for spectacular dances. It was also in Sitka, the old capital, that the Americans first hoisted the flag when they bought Alaska from Russia on 18 October 1867.

The purchase of Alaska was negotiated by William Seward – it cost America just $7,200,000 – and in the early years the huge land was frequently described as Seward's Folly or Seward's Icebox. But the following years were to bring wealth and great changes. Gold was discovered beneath the ground, bringing prospectors and adventurers to replace trappers and disturb the tranquility. Small towns sprang up, much as they sprang up

The earthquake in Anchorage on Good Friday 1964 moved 50,000 square miles. The tidal wave which followed drowned twelve people in California.

(Over page) Whaling boats have American style rig and hull design, but no motor, as the noise coming through the water would disturb the whales.

23

Peoples of Alaska

Alaskan Eskimo like this man originate from Central Asia. They never marry Indians, their traditional enemies who are of similar stock.

in America's west. Indians were killed or persuaded to join in the American bonanza. Even Eskimo, in the far north and the Arctic regions where they had hardly been disturbed for centuries, met the white men.

The Eskimo, it is believed, first came to Alaska about 6,000 years ago. They came from Asia by way of the Bering Strait – the same route by which the ancestors of the Indians had come, thousands of years before. Archaeologists have unearthed fishing lures, combs and harpoon points carved from bones and antlers, even walrus ivory etched with a scene showing Eskimo on a whale hunt. These date far back into Alaska's pre-history. Tiny blades of chert, a flint-like quartz, about an inch long and razor sharp have also been found, and identical blades have also been discovered around Lake Baikal in Siberia. These demonstrate that people in Asia and America have long been in contact with one another. And today the Eskimo are the most numerous of Alaska's indigenous people, inhabiting the coasts of the Bering Sea, the high Arctic, Little Diomede Island, and the Yukon and Kuskokwim river deltas.

Alaska's busiest Eskimo town is Barrow, far above the Arctic Circle. It faces onto the Arctic Ocean on a wind-swept bight of black gravel and here Eskimo have known of the outside world for more than a century – ever since New England whaling ships began to venture into the Arctic ocean. In summer the sun does not set for 82 days. Most of the 1,300 people are Eskimo and although they may work at other jobs many still depend on hunting and fishing for their livelihood. Here, also, Eskimo is the main language.

Kotzebue is another Eskimo town, facing onto the Chukchi Sea, where hunters on the beach hang up caribou antlers in the breeze, or butcher a freshly caught white whale, or skin a seal beside racks of rich red salmon. Small snow-covered huts line the road up from the beach, a few shacks made of packing cases and driftwood are covered with sod, and skins stretched out on the roofs to be dried. Here Eskimo women sometimes fish through holes in the ice close to the shore, wearing mittens and using sticks to manipulate the lines baited with a piece of walrus tusk shaped like a fish. Hunters stand around waiting, dressed in the warm fur parkas, khaki trousers and caribou *mukluk* shoes. The faces of many old Eskimo are lined and wrinkled, and the eyes seem no more than cracks in the skin, from a lifetime of squinting against the sun on the endless white snow.

Kotzebue was first established as a missionary settlement less than 100 years ago. Before that it was only a summer camp where Eskimo from the coast met others from inland to barter, to fish and to dance. In 1897 the missionaries came and built the first wooden frame house, which became the church. Whereas before the people had been nomadic on endless migrations, they now began to settle. They dug holes in the frozen ground, piled up logs of driftwood into walls and covered all with layers of sod. Now the houses are better constructed. But the dogs are still there, chained at night to every house, and in the day on the beach. Through the long winter they are needed to pull the sleds on hunting expeditions. At Christmas, hunters may go out into the tundra to bring back a caribou carcass buried in the snow since the fall. A ring of human footprints around the cache often keeps the wolves away, and if the hunter is gone for several days he will sleep in a caribou sleeping bag without a tent, eat frozen meat and drink water melted from ice by lighting a fire of willow twigs – just as the Eskimo has done for centuries. Even if, in some of these Eskimo towns, the language is lost, many of the old skills are not.

Nome, a town of 2,500 people, lies on the south coast of the Cape Prince of Wales. Some 80 per cent of its people are Eskimo, mainly King Island Eskimo. But its claim to fame lies in its gold rush history, a glamor so recent that there are still people alive to speak of it. Though the gleam is no longer apparent, and the shape of the town has changed at least twice from being destroyed by fire and flood, there is still an atmosphere of the old days between the boardwalks and the Bering

Sea. People still pan for gold, even though the giant dredges sit idle as though waiting for the days when interest in gold (and there is much speculation about what is left in the Seward peninsula and the possibilities of tapping gold from beneath the shallow sea) is revived.

The Eskimo did not start coming to Nome from their home on King island until after the town was established by Americans. At first they came in skin boats and set up summer camps on the beach for fishing, returning to their island in the winter. Now they are close to schools, hospitals and work. Yet even though the Eskimo here were isolated until fairly recently, a still smaller community of Eskimo would give a better picture of their way of life. Such a place is Napaskiak, further south, on the Kuskokwim river where there is only one American among 140 or so Eskimo (a few of whom are of Eskimo-American parents). Most consider themselves Yupik or pure Eskimo and feel closely akin to other Eskimo of adjacent Kuskokwim river villages. Contact with these other villages, and with the town of Bethel, are sporadic and depend almost entirely on the demands of hunting, fishing and the church – which is Russian Orthodox, and centered at a village called Russian Mission.

By December in Napaskiak the ground is covered in snow. The whiteness has also drifted along the river banks, around the overturned boats near the slough and piled up to the window level of most houses. The village is quiet and the only sign of life is the thin smoke which drifts upwards from the stove-pipes. Most of the houses are entered through a dark, cold storage shed where a white washing-machine often stands in one corner, a child's sled is propped up in another, and an outboard motor stands in a third. On shelves around the walls, dried, headless and filleted king salmon the shade of clotted blood are stored. Along the wall that forms part of the house fur parkas and jackets hang on nails.

The living area of the house is a single room about 18 feet square. At each of the three windows are cotton curtains hung on a string; there is the wood-burning stove, a metal-framed double bed with perhaps a home-made child's bed at its foot. Wooden chairs are gathered round a table that stands between the stove and the bed. In this one room the whole Eskimo family, mother, father and two or more children cook, eat, and sleep.

On a midwinter morning the room is perhaps 20° below freezing. At about 8 o'clock the man rises from his bed and lights the stove by adding shavings of dry spruce. He fills a kettle and places it on the stove, and then he returns to bed. The room is soon warm and the frost vanishes from the windows, and beads of moisture form beneath the waterline of the water-tank. Then his wife rises, dresses and turns to the stove to prepare coffee, bread and margarine. The children are dressed and given their breakfast. The man is ready to go outside where the thermometer reveals the temperature

Eskimo harpoon fishing tackle includes a coil of walrus-skin rope secured by a *baleen*, or soft whalebone thong.

(Bottom) A skilled hunter of Barrow, north-west Alaska, wields a whaling dart-gun from a boat made of sealskin bound to a frame by thongs.

is 30° below freezing. He puts dry grass insoles into his boots, puts on two pairs of socks, and covers his hands with gloves from the drying rack above the stove. He puts on his quilted parka in the storm shed outside, takes an axe from the chopping block and walks beyond the house to where the dogs are tethered.

As soon as the man leaves the house the dogs begin to yelp and scratch the ground in anticipation. He harnesses the dogs to the sled and heads out along the trail inland. They presently arrive at a cluster of tall, straight alders and there he loads the sled with nine-foot lengths of the wood. The sled bursts off along the trail again, back towards the village, passing on the way rabbit traps set a few days before. Back at the house, he spends a half-hour cutting the logs into stove lengths and then guides the dog-team and sled across the river to Oscarville, a tiny village with a store. On his return his wife sets out the midday meal.

The afternoon is spent hauling gallon cans of water to the house from a hole he has cut in the river ice. He builds a fire beneath an oil drum after unharnessing and chaining the team and cooks dried salmon backbones for the dogs. Before leaving the fire for a while he adds a pile of alder wood to make sure the fish are well cooked. 27

A white Beluga whale is spotted, and Eskimo paddle towards it, disregarding danger from the cake ice and from the prey itself.

(Center) The whale is harpooned. A walrus ivory etching has been found proving that Eskimo hunted whales in prehistoric times.

For two hours or so, in the afternoon, the man takes to the bath house with a kettle of warm water and by the time he is finished it is almost dark. He feeds the dogs and goes back into the house. He removes his boots and hangs his socks up over the stove to dry. The evening meal consists of blackfish. His wife pulls one at a time from a pan, squeezes the neck until the head makes a popping sound and then tosses it into the kettle. When the kettle is almost full, she adds a little water and sets it on the stove to simmer. During the remainder of the evening several friends may come to visit. A brother-in-law drops in to borrow a couple of dogs in order to haul a heavy load of fish from a cache in the tundra. The family listen to the radio. The man runs through a catalogue of guns. The children fall asleep on the large bed and have to be undressed by their mother.

In summer the mornings are lighter and the family rises earlier. Salmon fishing dominates much of the day and evening for the men, sitting in the boat with gill nets, waiting for the run. Or there may be a film show in Oscarville which almost everyone from the surrounding villages comes to, tugged there by the children. Afterwards, when the children have fallen asleep and been put to bed, the man may again take himself out to the river to net more salmon. Sometimes the men fish until early morning, when they return to the village, unload the catch, cover the boat with canvas and stroll home to bed.

Napaskiak is a community where children are universally desired and numerically the largest section of the population. A childless couple are pitied, for

Villagers help pull in the 40-ton whale, which will provide meat, four types of cooking and fuel oil, candle fat and bone boat thwarts.

Muktuk (white skin and blubber) flensed from the white whale, will be pickled. Had it been from a blowhead whale it would have been frozen.

(Center) Cut in pieces, the whale lies on the beach at Barrow. Every member of the whaling crew gets an even share of the kill.

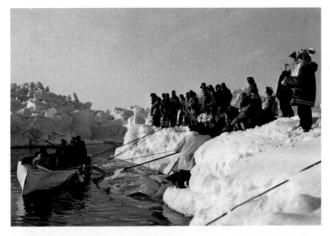

Whale meat, cut by a saw with an enormous blade, goes quickly into an ice cellar dug from the permafrost. It will be eaten slightly high.

children are enjoyed throughout their youth, and later come to support their parents. The birth of the first child often ends the turbulent domestic relations of so many newly-weds. The mother of a new-born child is the center of attraction. The father is envied, especially if he has a son. If the first child is a girl someone is likely to say to the father 'What's wrong? Can't you make a boy?' There is an undeniable pressure on both parents not only to have children, but also to make sure the first is a boy. Then, there is added pressure to produce still more children. The infant mortality rate, however, is high. In one period of two years out of eleven children born, only seven survived.

The routine of daily village life may at times seem to be a series of monotonous repetitions, especially in the depths of winter when there is only little activity. At other times of the year, as with the approach of long summer days, life again becomes purposeful, filled with activity. But it is the behavior of the people toward one another in these everyday activities which best describes the nature of their community. The social life rests upon the foundation of mutual obligations, binding fathers and sons into a network of responsibilities. Their life-long association is not overtly warm or friendly, but it is one of mutual respect. A young son may be bashful and retiring in front of his father, and this same attitude lingers into adult life when the grown man stares out of a window as his aged father speaks to him. It is characteristic that neither will condemn or praise the other face to face; and a father is nevertheless indulgent towards his growing son even if the boy does not quickly realize his duties. To criticize the boy openly would offend and alienate him, and that is avoided.

A son grows up helping his father support the family. He fishes with his father, hunts with his father and turns over to his father all the pelts he has taken. Likewise he gives his father the money he has earned from wage labor. Even after the son is married this implicit sub-ordination continues. And yet the tradition that requires a son to care for his ageing father now comes to have less and less meaning. There are old-age pensions for the fathers which make them less dependent on their sons. It is, perhaps, the first time that these men have had steady incomes, and often they are able to maintain a higher standard of living than their offspring. The impact of this innovation is, as yet, only slight. The villagers seem unaware of how radical this change might prove.

An adult woman in the community who has lost her husband through death or divorce has lost her formal means of support. She is, however, helped by her relatives and by the Bureau of Indian Affairs. Such a woman is also likely to be regarded as an eligible sexual partner for both unmarried and married village men. (This is not to say that such village women are promiscuous.) It is probable that a man who has an 29

(Left) Eskimo women fish through an ice-hole, playing the frozen line with sticks and using a feather as float. They harpoon seals at similar holes.

Underneath the wooden fishing boat traditionally belonging to the women is an ivory runner for crossing ice fields.

affair with a widow or a divorcée will make her gifts of clothing or food; but this is not a real obligation. Before the organization of government relief programs, aid from transient lovers was probably far more important than it is now. A mild stigma may attach to the child of an unmarried mother and villagers will speculate on which man the child resembles. But should the mother later marry, the child and any others are readily accepted by the new husband.

In Napaskiak there are two practising shamans, one an old man, the other a young girl. The old man is regarded with trust by most of the villagers; he is able to predict the future and cure aching limbs. The girl can also do these things but people have less faith in her abilities. The old shaman is a member of the Russian Orthodox Church and at the same time he was a shaman he was also a church leader. Some in the village will denounce him as a fraud, but others will seek his aid whenever they have sprains, sores or other illnesses. Patients do not have to pay for his services, but they do give him gifts. And the shaman himself does not suggest that a sick man should try his methods alone. When the shaman was ill he did not hesitate to take penicillin shots from the village teacher to aid his recovery.

In this Eskimo community, the dead only deserve particular attention from the living immediately following death and at certain other remembrance ceremonies. In the normal routine of daily life the dead do not impose on their relatives. But each person is believed to have a spirit or soul which survives him after death, and this must be satisfied that all is well with near relatives in order to remain peacefully in heaven. But these beliefs are founded essentially on the Russian Orthodox teachings; they are not shamanistic, for the shamans have a highly respectful attitude towards the church. The merits and sins of a man's life are weighed by God and decide his passage to heaven or hell.

Immediately after someone dies all the windows and doors of the house are opened so that the soul may depart. After the burial everything is shut to prevent the soul's return, for a ghost may come back with malicious intent. A small icon is hung over the door to prevent a return through that passage. Then, if a soul or ghost disapproves of the behavior of the living, it may return to haunt them. In one situation a dead man's sons made too much noise in the house and the father's ghost returned to make noises outside on the porch. One of the sons had to drive it back to the grave with a knife. But if a ghost should touch someone that person is sure to die soon after. At Easter time, it is believed, there are many ghosts around and the people paint crosses inside the house over the windows and doors to keep them away. The Orthodox Church is the most complex institution in Napaskiak and its services and ritual obligations draw villagers together throughout the year. But although the church unites the villagers, it is itself only partly inte-

Walrus must be killed on the ice before they can reach the sea, since their corpses sink. Experienced Eskimo hunters do not shoot them in the water.

(Center) Hunters approach sleeping walrus on a cake of ice. When one finally wakes, its alarm signal prompts a volley of shots.

31

Peoples of Alaska

The skin of the freshly killed Bering Sea seal is made into a bag to contain its flesh, sinews and intestines.

Alaska has always attracted adventurous men, including preachers, who have converted many natives and settlers in its rough, desolate territory.

grated with the rest of village life.

To make a living in this community demands that a man has many divers skills. It is not enough to be a good trapper, for there are years when the fur animals are scarce or the market is overloaded. Neither is it enough to be just a good fisherman, for at times the fish do not run and there are few to be caught. A man has to be both trapper and hunter, fisherman and craftsman. Through the long spring and summer days he has to work hard; he must also be able to adjust to times of inactivity, particularly in mid-winter when the temperature is down, the winds are sometimes high and food resources almost inaccessible.

Following the freeze up around November the ice is thick enough to carry a man across the river. At first he walks cautiously, carrying a long-handled ice-pick before him, testing the ice. At this time there are usually several men already established at their trapping camps on the tundra to the south east of the village. They take their dogs and sleds with them, mink-traps, dried fish and other supplies. There is much traffic over the river ice, back and forth carrying blackfish back to the village. As the snow thickens everywhere there is activity; cutting alders for firewood, shooting the last ducks and geese, fishing through holes in the ice for pike and lush. At the camps in the tundra the men set up their traps at the entrance to mink holes; they shoot ptarmigan when they have the opportunity. Each mink pelt will bring in about $25, and before the trapping begins most men will have obtained credit from the traders. From the end of January to the beginning of March there is little activity. The men haul firewood, hunt ptarmigan, trap rabbits. By late winter most families are relying on the previous summer's salmon catch as their staple food. In April, however, ptarmigan arrive in huge flocks around the

Sealskins are stretched onto a frame to dry and be cleaned. They are then used to make kayaks, sails, and rugs and hangings for the home.

(Right) Constant exposure to Arctic temperatures and weathering has made this St Lawrence island woman's face as tough as her hide parka.

Caribou legs hang to dry. The skins nailed on the outside wall will be used to make *mukluks*, the Eskimo's long heavy-duty boots.

Diced white Beluga whalemeat hangs from this winter food drying rack, out of reach of grizzly bear and dogs. Skins are spread out in front of it.

At Tuktoyaktuk in the Mackenzie area, raw bearskins cost 70 dollars each. The annual bear kill from each settlement is limited.

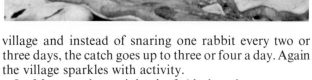

village and instead of snaring one rabbit every two or three days, the catch goes up to three or four a day. Again the village sparkles with activity.

In May on the mainland of Alaska, there are vast differences in natural conditions. This is not merely because of the extent of the country from north to south, but also because a great part of the interior belongs to the temperate forest zone. New green leaves show on the birch trees at the end of May, just as they do in New England in the middle of April. Around Anchorage, which is really not very far from the Arctic, spring brings with it a whole new color and a fresh world. Millions of mosquitoes have already begun their torment of men and animals. This is the so called 'Arctic terror' of which so much has been said in the stories of the old days from gold prospectors.

In May the Nunamiut, or inland Eskimo who live within the Arctic circle, are out in their tents discovering the warm sun of spring. Snow melts across the slopes of valleys, and brooks become waterways once more. Heather and willows spring to life, birds sing from the willowy scrub. Flocks of geese make their way north, gulls sail over the valley on white wings. And here the caribou come from the south, passing by in a hurry to reach the places where their calves will be born – places where mosquitoes will not torment the tender skin of the new-born. The males and females of the herds migrate separately and everywhere the ravens can be seen following the females.

The ravens are very cunning birds. They know that the males do not give birth to calves, and they know also that when a mother gives birth she leaves the young animal for two or three days during which the calf does not move since it is too weak to walk. It would be easy prey for wolves and wolverines. The calves resemble stones and it is said they give off no scent that might attract carnivorous animals. If the mother stayed close by the calf would move, try to stand up and so be exposed. Thus the mother leaves it, and it is only the ravens who know where to look. They swoop down and with their sharp bills savage the caribou calves. The Alaska wilderness is both beautiful and wild. The caribou are also prey for the Nunamiut.

What the buffalo were to the plains Indians, the caribou were to the Indian nomads of the far north. The Indians in Alaska did not live beyond the Arctic circle but ranged throughout the forest zone between the Yukon and the Mackenzie. In southern Alaska their close contacts with Eskimo meant that they acquired many Eskimo cultural traits. The Indians here, like the Nunamiut who ranged through the mountains to the west, were also nomads. In the early summer months the Indian tribes fished for food and hunted caribou and moose later on and in the winter.

The Athapascan were one such group of tribes, though today there are only a few thousand left. For

An island enclosure at Tigara Point Hope, where Eskimo are often put in large clapboard coffins above ground, for a Christian style 'burial'.

(Bottom) Permafrost on St Lawrence island prevents burial, and scavengers take their fill of the corpses in the Eskimo graveyard.

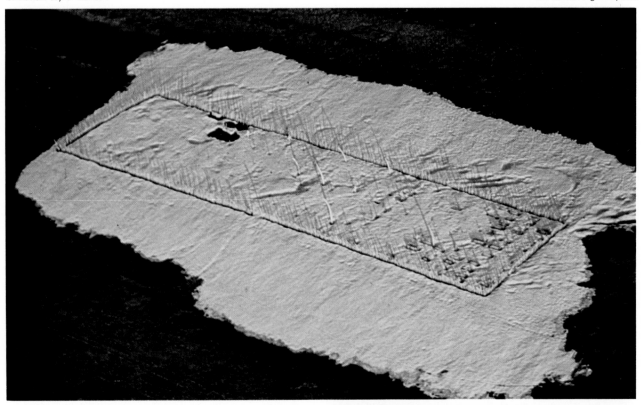

them hunting was a communal affair. They howled like wolves and drove the herds into the funnel of a pound. Then the hunters blocked the entrance and shot the animals with arrows as they tried to escape. They and other Indians also hunted individually, stalking moose or caribou with their bows and arrows. Magic was often a preliminary to the hunt. One method was to use the shoulder blade of a caribou, etched with images of the animal, held over a fire until it cracked in the heat. The cracks indicated the direction in which good hunting would be found, and also told whether or not the hunt would be successful.

When large quantities of meat or fish were taken in the summer, much was dried on racks and smoked. It was then stored in baskets of birchbark and kept for the lean seasons. In winter the frozen ground provided a natural deep-freeze where meat could be preserved in pits. The food was easily cooked in containers of bark or skin filled with water. The water was brought to the boil merely by the addition of hot stones. In summer the winter log cabins were left behind as the tribe moved off after the caribou. During those months they lived in dome-shaped tents covered with skins. They carried everything on sleds drawn by the women. Women also had to retrieve game killed by the hunters and bring it back to camp. They made all the clothing, repaired snowshoes and did virtually all the drudgery of the camp. Like the Eskimo and the Aleut in the Aleutian

35

Peoples of Alaska

The Nuliarig Alaskans used to
believe that their drum dance,
performed with wooden masks,
parkas and chanting, could
heal the sick.

Eskimo have a great
respect for the Russian
Orthodox church, especially in
the once Russian
Pribilof islands.

Islands, the Indians in Alaska made the most of the wilderness. And in the shadow of the massive Mount McKinley with its peak always white with the snow, where glaciers still creep through high valleys, the Alaska which those people knew is being changed.

One hundred and fifty miles north-east of Mount McKinley lies Fairbanks, reputedly the Golden Heart of Alaska. From its beginnings until the 1930s the name was appropriate, for this was once a gold rush boom town. Today, with the dredges idle and with the remaining gold there panned largely for fun, Fairbanks prospers because of oil and air travel. Many Alaskans use airplanes like city-dwellers use taxis. And the town is conveniently placed both for this service and also as a supply point for oil fields of the north Slope. Here memories of the wild old days are almost lost beneath the frenzy of Alaska's development. And it is not only oil which brings prosperity to this town of 30,000 people, with its weathered frame shops wedged between glistening concrete buildings. The long arm of tourism has reached into Alaska, so that visitors now bring in more money than the prospectors, 70 years ago, ever took out.

Only 11 miles outside Fairbanks an entire town has been preserved for visitors to remind them of the old days. It is called Cripple Creek and was once a company-owned mining town called Ester. Like a ghost town, but without the ghosts, Cripple Creek preserves an old saloon, a hotel and even a gold mine. Yet without the rough, rowdy atmosphere which once possessed so many towns in the gold rush era, Cripple Creek is just a little too soft for some tastes. There are thousands of Americans who yearn for something of the spirit of adventure of frontier life. And for these people Alaska can still offer a solution.

In the snow-covered forests that spread out around Mount McKinley, where in winter there are ice-covered lakes every ten miles, Alaskan-Americans have settled in log cabins not merely as holiday retreats, but as permanent homes. Their nearest neighbors are often ten-foot grizzly bears. They build caches for their meat on top of 20-foot poles. They insulate their cabins against the terrific cold of winter and strengthen them against gales and 15-foot snow drifts. And they live by hunting, by working as guides on hunting-trips or even as laborers on rail or road building projects. It is not a unique way of life. The Indians and the Eskimo lived much like this for centuries, but to these Americans it offers a new opportunity to attune themselves to a real wilderness.

Alaska has always made real demands on her people. Even if today some of those demands are easily overcome by such things as central heating (which anyway is restricted to certain towns) and airplanes, the difficulties are real enough. An expedition across the winter snows, with crevasses to look out for, can lead to disaster and will often leave frost-bite scars. Just a short distance from the comfort of cities like Fairbanks, Alaska makes all the rules. And it is this vision of Alaska which persists. A volcano or an earthquake is a rare reminder. The coldness of the winter is perennial.

Today the old hunters speak of an alarming reduction in the herds of moose and caribou. Homesteaders who have settled in log cabins are unhappy about the trans-Alaska oil pipe-line which seems to be imminent. Though the project will double the present income of the state, placing oil far above fishing as the major industry, the long-term advantages are doubtful. Some say it is the beginning of the end of the Alaskan wilderness. Even back in the 1930s a similar comment was being made. Robert Marshall, an early explorer of the Brooks range in Alaska, wrote in 1938: 'Alaska is unique among all recreational areas belonging to the United States because Alaska is yet largely a wilderness. In the name of a balanced use of American resources, let's keep northern Alaska largely a wilderness.' Even since that time much has happened to change parts of the Alaskan wilderness forever.

North Pacific Haida Indians
dance at Saxman before totems
embodying their ancestors and
other spirits who watch
everything they do.

Eskimo used to make figures
for their own sake, or to
appeal to spirits. Now white
people have made them
conscious of an Eskimo art.

Arctic diggers and explorers

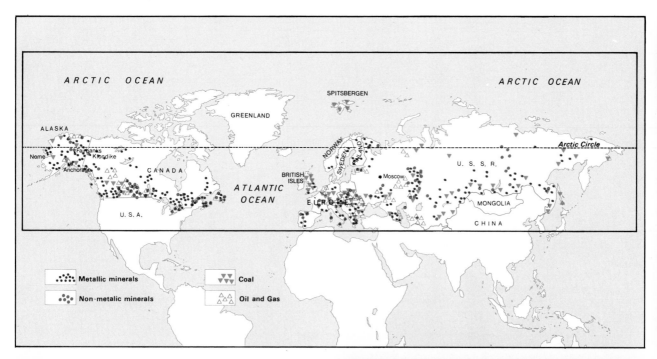

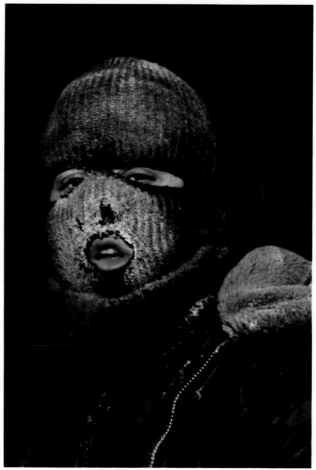

No region in the world has so successfully lured adventurers into her desolate wastelands at such perilous risk and for so slender a chance of reward. Yet the Arctic has for centuries tempted Americans and Europeans – from Irish monks to Cossacks – to wander into her circle and try to discover her icily guarded secrets. Nowadays modern commercial enterprises and governments have decided that there are definite financial and strategic rewards to be won from the Arctic, and they have minimized the physical, if not mental, human risks. Nevertheless, it is still surprising that men will sacrifice years of their lives to the comfortless Arctic.

There are men, warmed by the ancient pioneer spirit who still brave the blank frozen landscape single-handed in the hope of asserting their mastery over the terrain, even if they do not benefit from it financially.

There are still Arctic adventurers who choose to spend their winter months in the solitary darkness of the extreme north. If they live to see the sunrise, as men solemnly call the end of winter, their minds, if not their bodies, may have 'frozen up'. Nevertheless, men considered far from mad have for centuries plodded into the high Arctic, and of those who have returned many have apparently stayed sane.

Arctic adventurers have had two main motives. Some have desired wealth – from whales, furs, gold and, today, from a wide variety of minerals. Some have desired fame – the accolade due to the first man on the North Pole, or the first to travel the North-west Passage and the admiration due to those who can brave and master the worst that nature can offer. Many have desired both, but

The 'black gold' of oil has turned out far more valuable than the gold diggers ever dreamed. It gives the Arctic a world-wide importance.

Prudhoe Bay mining area
relies on Fairbanks for all
supplies and airlifts. The
Hercules aircraft have sometimes
crash-landed in 60 mph blizzards.

39

Drilling is continuous. Motors
must always be kept running
to avoid freezing, but inside
the prefabricated shacks the
heating is formidable.

Arctic diggers and explorers

Climbing a rig needs a safety harness. Oilmen in Alaska work a daily twelve hour shift for three months, and then take six weeks off.

(Bottom) The 'Cat Train' snow plows a pioneer route through the Brooks range, which spans Alaska above the Arctic Circle.

few have won either.

In the 4th century BC a Greek sailor named Pytheas reached Thule in north-west Greenland. In the 8th century AD Irish monks settled in Iceland. About a hundred years later Vikings established colonies in Greenland, and pushed on northwards. But it was only to their shallow graves that they carried all their knowledge of the Arctic.

In the Middle Ages it was Spanish and Portuguese control of the warmer sea-routes of the world that persuaded the English and other Europeans to search for the North-west and North-east Passages and the way to Cathay and all its fabulous riches. From 1553 the Englishmen Willoughby and Chancellor attempted to force the North-east Passage. The English traded with Murmansk and Archangel. The Muscovy Company flourished and furs came to west Europe. But ships could only manage brief summer excursions into the ice-blocked northern seas. The ruthless horsebound nomads, the Cossacks, had more success than the sailors. They reached the Pacific in the 17th century. Of the sailors only the Dane, Vitus Bering, employed by Peter the Great of Russia managed real advances along the North-east Passage. In 1741 he crossed the strait named after him. But the world had to wait nearly forty years for Captain Cook to establish for certain that the Bering Strait existed.

The North-west Passage was even more elusive. From 1576 onwards Britons – first Martin Frobisher, who mistakenly thought he had discovered gold, then William John Davis, who brought dancers and music with him in order to endear the Eskimo – tried to round the North American continent. Henry Hudson, the name adopted by the Hudson's Bay Company, reached a record latitude of 80° 23″ north and made a fortune out of whales, but in 1610 his crew mutinied and set him with his small son and a few loyalists adrift in the icy waters, never to be heard of again. In 1773 Captain Phipps, with the then 14 year old Horatio Nelson on board, surpassed Hudson's record. In 1818 the British passed an Act of Parliament offering £20,000 ($50,000) for the discovery of the North-west Passage, and £5,000 ($12,500) for the attainment of the North Pole. The disappearance of the English Arctic explorer Sir John Franklin in 1845 aroused even more interest in the Passage than before, and Americans joined the hunt. In 1850 McClure unwittingly went through the Passage, partly by ship and partly on foot, then had to be rescued. But it was the American explorer Captain McClintock who confirmed the reality of the Passage three years later and ended the hope that it might be a regular commercial route. In 1903 the Norwegian Roald Amundsen, in a tiny yacht, was the first to navigate it.

It was even harder to reach the Pole. Whereas the South Pole, where even colder temperatures are recorded, is on a secure solid land mass rising in places to a great

The vast tundra is barren whether under snow or not. In the frozen north there are few animals, and only sparse scrub around the mining camp.

height (hence the coldness), the North Pole is on a treacherously moving ice-pack. The Arctic is not all motionless silence. There is continuous movement. There are several layers of water of varying temperature under the ice which is slowly drifting. Ice-sheets run into each other causing pressure ridges, sometimes fifteen feet high, to pile up. Sometimes the movements cause the ice to crack apart, opening up wide 'leads' impossible to cross. All this is accompanied by creaking and cracking sounds. Sometimes explorers have found themselves stranded on gyrating ice islands.

A Norwegian scholar named Fridtjof Nansen made a revolutionary discovery. He recognized that this Arctic drift could be exploited. He put his theory to the test in 1893, and drifted across the Arctic icecap in his especially pliable ship *Fram*. (Modern steel ships have always suffered from their lack of flexibility against the powerful swell and contraction of the ice). Nansen successfully drifted for almost three years, but passed further from the Pole than he anticipated – and failed in his attempt to find it.

The first man to reach the Pole was probably the American Lieutenant Robert Peary with a negro driver and two Eskimo in April 1909, but his compatriot Dr Cook claimed to have achieved the feat a year earlier. Cook's claims are doubted by many, and controversy still rages around the two men. The Americans Byrd and Bennet flew to the Pole in 1926, beating Amunsen and Nobile by two days. In 1958 the US submarine *Nautilus* sailed directly under the Pole. But it was not until 1968 that a British team led by Wally Herbert made the first surface crossing of Arctic on ice from one side to the other.

The Norwegian Stefansson's concept of a Pole of Relative Inaccessibility, a point that is about 450 miles on the Alaskan side of the true Pole, meant another target for explorers to reach, and one more elusive even than the Pole itself.

Exploration was usually bound up with financial (and later scientific) goals, but the search for the Pole was almost purely a matter of prestige. The probings of North-west passagers and Siberian Cossacks mingled the motives. As well as simple adventurers, there were whalers and furriers too. Cossacks had a lucrative trade in furs from Yakut tribesmen whose marksmanship was so good they would shoot their prey in the eye, leaving its skin unmarked (Yakut later became top Red Army marksmen).

The mad Klondike Gold Rush of 1896 must have been the acme of sheer thirst for riches. The Klondike river runs into the Yukon river in the far north-west of Canada. For about 800 square miles around the confluence of the two rivers, rich gold-bearing gravels were found by lone pioneers – trappers, fur dealers, panners. The high quality of the find at the Bonanza creek lured 30,000 hopeful searchers into the area, and within **41**

In summer the sea off north Alaska is navigable but ice often has to be broken. A long pipeline is planned to take the oil to the US refineries.

42

Black Mike, who claims to be over a century old, is one of the few Gold Rush pioneers left in Dawson City, and a sourdough, or winter veteran.

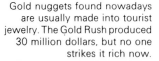

Dawson City, like many other Klondike settlements, is only a ghost of its boomtown days. Its population, 50,000 around 1900, is now about 800.

Gold nuggets found nowadays are usually made into tourist jewelry. The Gold Rush produced 30 million dollars, but no one strikes it rich now.

months every acre was staked out. Men trekked over 2,000 miles in their snow shoes, usually to find they were too late. Well stocked gold-seekers callously passed by the unluckier ones who lay by the roadside freezing and starving. There were many oneway footprints and little charity. Diseases of the white man decimated the Indians. Winter, especially, was hard, and men would eagerly await the first geese overhead and the noisy breakup of the river ice. Some of the Klondike people were old hands. Since the days of Henry Hudson and the first remote 'factories' (as they were called) on the lakes and rivers, many rival companies had sprung up, and men like Alexander Mackenzie, first to travel the whole way down to the river named after him and into the sea, worked for them. But most Klondikers were greenhorns with only avarice, and no experience, to drive them on. By 1900 22 million dollars of gold had been found, but by 1906 they had collected only $5.6 million more. A few years later there was an exodus to Alaska, and Dawson, the once-thriving center of the Klondike became a ghost town.

Since throughout this region the ground was hard frozen, mines were worked by a thawing process, first by fire, later by steam. Much later hydraulic mining was introduced, and the last gold was dredged as late as 1966. Most of the time, mining was exhausting work and although Klondike was a boom for a handful, for most it was a tragedy. Names like Hell's Gate, Devil's Gorge, the Rapid of the Drowned testify to the ferocity of the climate. Mosquitoes, scurvy, starvation, the high risk of accident, the spectacle of men stewing their mocassins for food – these were the all too frequent rewards of the Klondike.

The word Arctic comes from the Greek *arktos*, meaning the bear. The ancients named the most northern constellation after it. The most popular definition is probably 'the land and sea north of latitude 66° 30′ N, where the sun does not set on midsummer's day. Others say, where the treeline ends, there the Arctic begins. Thus some places would be Arctic while others further north might not. And the treeless north coasts of

Hydraulic dredging, the last and most effective way the Yukon was mined, has scarred the river bed with trailing piles of sludge.

43

Arctic diggers and explorers

The Gold Rush saw queues like
this one in the Chilkout pass
in 1898 for staking claims.
Falling out of line meant a
long wait to rejoin.

Labrador and Iceland would just qualify. Still others say that the Arctic begins where Indians refuse to live and Eskimo thrive. The presence of permafrost – where the ground never thaws out – is the yardstick of others. This again would make latitude irrelevant, and Siberia would become the largest Arctic land mass.

Permafrost seriously affects human life, for the building of houses, roads and railways over permafrost is dangerous: if the frost beneath thaws out, swellings and sometimes even large bubbles appear and destroy the foundations. Only to archaeologists is permafrost useful: many mammoths have been found in perfect condition in permafrost zones, some almost a million years old. Recently the New York Exploration Society had Alaskan mammoth's meat on the menu of its annual dinner.

If the Arctic is too cold for most humans, it is too cold for most animals as well. There are, however, fluctuations in the climate. For instance, Greenland in the Middle Ages proved too harsh for sheep, though they survive there happily now. The walrus is almost extinct now, but if one of the rare survivors should hook its tusks over the gunwhales of your boat, as one did to Nansen's *Fram*, you should gently unhook them: they are fierce and strong. Eskimo depended on the fat of seals, but few white men in the Arctic followed suit. There are many reindeer farms in Siberia and Arctic Scandinavia, and people eat the caribou as well, though they cannot domesticate it. They hunt the musk ox, though they trail it with difficulty, as the long shaggy hair of its belly blurs its footprints. Other animals that give but scant meat to Arctic people are the polar wolf (who fears man's best friend in the Arctic, the husky dog), the Arctic fox, the lemming, and the Arctic hare. Most famous of all Arctic animals is the Polar bear, whose low yellowish shape (they get up on their hind legs to defend themselves) ambling purposefully towards the camp has put fear into the hearts of explorers for centuries. The bears are powerful, inquisitive, unafraid, and rarely aggressive. In the summer, mosquitoes infuriate men in the southern Arctic, but otherwise insects are few.

Anyone traveling in the Arctic knows how precious the sledge dog is. They are superior to the reindeer in the worst conditions, for reindeer are too fussy about their food, demanding too much of that special moss that is unavailable in the remote Arctic. Sledge dogs have a stamina only comparable to wolves, and the two species are doubtless related. It is said husky breeders crossed dogs with wolves by leaving the bitch tied to a tree believing a wolf father increases the pup's stamina. Huskies can be ferocious dogs too, but rarely cannibalistic. They shun the meat of a dead brother when they are hungry, as many explorers know. No Arctic traveler can afford to be sentimental. In number, dog teams vary between five and fifteen, male and female. Some drivers

Though men rarely co-operated in the Gold Rush, it was in everyone's interest to clear the railroad when blizzards struck on the Yukon route.

(Center) Miners crossed the windswept glacier Crater Lake into Dawson City without any trouble. Glaciers cover 20,000 square miles, or 3% of Alaska.

In 1896 Klondike tent settlements such as Lindeman sprang up within months. Many arrived too late to stake a claim and moved on to Alaska.

like to have a bitch in the lead to excite and encourage the dogs, and also so that when she has pups they can learn their job running beside their mother. In Arctic Eurasia dogs are often castrated. Old dogs though weaker often do best, because they pull more steadily. Young ones often go too fast and tire quickly.

In the eastern Arctic drivers like to have their dogs each on a separate lead fanned out in front, which is well adapted to open tundra or sea ice. Western Arctic drivers prefer their dogs to run tandem, two by two.

Huskies will rarely fail you, while machinery often will. Nonetheless, even in Greenland, Canada and Alaska, where they are most common, more and more men are beginning to use the modern means of transport. In the Arctic USSR life is far more technologically geared and people live little different from their compatriots further south. Ordinary people in the West barely consider the Russians an Arctic people, though in fact the USSR's Arctic population far exceeds that of the rest of the Arctic put together. In land, Canada is the biggest owner, with 37 per cent, while USSR ties with Denmark (Greenland) for second place at 28 per cent, followed by US Alaska at 6 per cent. But the USSR has done far more to develop the Arctic's tremendous mineral wealth than any of her Arctic co-owners. The mythology of Arctic exploration and mineral seeking may be Canadian, American, Norwegian, Danish, British – but only Russia has more systematically tapped the Arctic potential.

In modern terms the Arctic is of less importance as a field for adventure or for the individual's search for fortune: her importance is now strategic, for wealth in minerals like oil which demand large scale mining operation. Furs were once called 'soft gold'; real gold is far more abundant in Arctic USSR than in Canada. Russians do have the added advantages of lesser glaciation and three navigable rivers – the Ob', Lena and Yenisey, all among the longest in the world. But they contend with colder temperatures, and the northern sea route (the North-east Passage) is navigable only three months of the year. Arctic USSR people live much as they do in Moscow. Five of their Arctic cities have populations of over 100,000.

Russian isolation after the Revolution forced the new régime to mine its own gold at great expense. Now USSR is second only to South Africa in production. The Arctic Yakutskaya and Indigarka-Kolyma mines produce 80· per cent of the country's gold. Mica, tin, tungsten, industrial diamonds and coal all come out of the Soviet Arctic. The large Arctic cities of Nickel and Norilsk produce a wealth of nickel, and there is tin and copper too.

In what scientists call 'non-renewable resources' the Russians are ahead as well. They have collectivized herds of reindeer. They use the taiga's virgin forests for timber. They still sell furs. And they are exploiting

Men tried without success to invent scoops, churns and conveyors to separate gold dust mechanically from dirt. Panning by hand was too slow.

Houses were built at Nome right on the beaches of the Seward peninsula where the gold had been found, and were repeatedly swept out to sea.

(Center) Even in the winter miners dug, thawing the ground with bonfires and steam. They claimed frozen mud, and waited until the thaw to wash it.

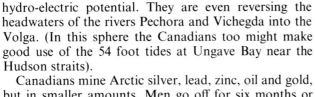

hydro-electric potential. They are even reversing the headwaters of the rivers Pechora and Vichegda into the Volga. (In this sphere the Canadians too might make good use of the 54 foot tides at Ungave Bay near the Hudson straits).

Canadians mine Arctic silver, lead, zinc, oil and gold, but in smaller amounts. Men go off for six months or yearly stints, into the industrial Canadian Arctic. There is little community life, although physical dangers have been overcome. Supplies are dropped regularly, and there are showers, driers, hand washing facilities. There are movies and record-players, but other diversions are few. Life is more a battle against boredom.

Today the Arctic is of crucial importance to international strategy. People have tended to think of the world as cylindrical: 'the top and bottom are small and unimportant'. In fact the Arctic today is as important a mediterranean as the Mediterranean sea was to the Ancient world. Canada's Cape Columbia is nearer to Moscow than to its capital city of Ottawa. So the Americans have spent many millions of dollars building a DEW (Direct Early Warning) Line in a 3,000 mile arc from west Alaska to Baffin Island. The Russians are equally aware of the Arctic as a line of defence or attack, and the military engineer has replaced the trapper. Life as an engineer in the Arctic is uneventful. Polar bears may harass the camp; if you peer too closely through the theodolite, your eyelid may freeze fast to the metal eyepiece. Doctors are not handy. You must take precautions against winteritis – the condition of the mind when it becomes blank from monotony and judgement is blurred. Little else happens.

Nevertheless, Russians and Americans and all Arctic white men alike experience the same unique feelings at some time or other. The pioneer spirit does occasionally break out of the technological straitjacket. Men are sometimes forced to take on nature at its worst and coldest, almost singlehanded. The bare essentials of life are what matters. How to oppose the cold? How to travel light, yet stay warm? Caribou parka jackets are best. Caribou hairs do moult slowly but the tiny cavity in each hair keeps the temperature more constant than other garments. String-vests work on the same principle, guarding pockets of air by the skin.

'Have no desires and you will be the richest man in the world' said Cervantes. When Arctic man is in trouble, food is his preoccupation. Hunger is by no means a safe measure of inadequacy, however. Calorie intake must be carefully checked, and different peoples apparently need varying amounts. Eskimo in Alaska have around 3,000 a day; Spitzberg miners 4,500; and hard-slogging British explorers over 6,000. Food dreams betray the wishes of the body – and the culinary fantasies usually revolve round protein and fat, especially fat. Palatability becomes secondary. The white man is reduced to his most fundamental, his humblest.

Often whole families went gold-digging. Here you could discover beforehand whether you were going to make your fortune.

47

Canadian Eskimo

Eskimo could not survive
without their dog teams. As
he travels, the man makes skin
'boots' to protect his dogs'
feet from the sharp ice.

Netsilik

Midwinter in Arctic Canada is extremely cold. The ice is up to seven feet thick. The temperature often drops to minus 40°F. The sun barely tops the horizon at its highest point and a twilight reigns in the few hours when it is not pitch dark. At such a time, about fifty years ago, one might have seen a solitary Netsilik hunter immobile in the sea snow, standing silently for hour upon hour in the dying daylight. He would be waiting at a seal's breathing hole to harpoon a seal in the split second as it came up for air. Netsilik means 'the people of the seal'.

High summer in the Arctic is short-lived. But at night the sun hardly disappears. The mossy tundra is carpeted in flowers. Hares, foxes and ptarmigan have lost their white winter camouflage to blend into the darker colors of summer. Waterfowl swim in the open lakes. At this time one might have seen a group of Netsilik shouting and laughing as they speared salmon trout at a river trap. Or one might have come across a patient couple stalking the caribou. Bent forwards pretending to graze, with their fur hoods covering their faces and bows and arrows held upwards like antlers they were imitating the caribou to get closer. Then suddenly up they would jump and shoot away their arrows.

The Netsilik are a small group of Eskimo who live in the north of Canada on the Boothia peninsula, a tongue of land reaching between King William island and Boothia gulf. In 1923 there were 259 of them. Their original hunting culture is now remembered only by a few old folk. But enough has been recorded for us to see how people survived in one of the harshest climates known to man, relying only on the raw materials to hand: snow and ice, skin, bone, stone and a little driftwood. Their technology was complex, their social organization simple. They wandered in small hunting bands over a large area. They were quick to laugh, slow to anger. By the Aivilik to the east, they were thought bellicose, coarse and slovenly. Their numbers, always in danger of diminishing through the natural hazards of their environment, were further threatened by a high rate of suicide and frequent cases of female infanticide.

The main changes in Netsilik culture began in the early years of this century as trading posts were established in the north. Iron was introduced and so were guns, making hunting easier and lessening the Netsilik's dependence on each other. Catholic and Protestant missionaries went there in the 1930s and converted them to Christianity. Now the Netsilik are concentrated in three main settlements; at Gjoa Haven on King William island, Spence bay and Kugardjuk on Pelly bay. There are government schools and nursing stations. Young Netsilik speak English, dress in western clothes, eat western food and use steel tools.

The Netsilik preyed on the animals around them. They had no crops and no domestic animals except for each family's few husky dogs. Life was divided into two parts: **49**

An igloo can be built very
quickly when the travelers
stop for the night. The ice
walls curve round in a
continuous spiral.

winter seal hunting on the sea ice and summer fishing and
caribou hunting inland. In winter they lived in igloos,
in summer they lived in sealskin tents. The host of
Netsilik taboos confirmed this duality. No work on
caribou skins was allowed at sealing camps. It was
strictly forbidden to eat trout or land animals on the day
one had eaten seal meat. Land and sea animals were
kept as separate as summer is from winter.

In late spring when the sea ice was almost melted the
Netsilik left their winter camps and moved onto the
mainland in little family groups. They made sealskin
tents and re-covered their kayaks. They left behind the
things they did not want – wooden sleds, dogs harnesses,
whips, drying racks, soapstone lamps, unnecessary
clothing, seal oil – and stored it on little islands or on
cliff tops well away from foxes and other predators. At
the beginning of July they were ready for their long trek
inland to the summer fishing camp, each one heavily
laden, for sleds were no good in the soft melting snow.

Salmon trout were caught as they swam, each year, up
the rivers from the sea. The biggest catches occurred at
the stone weirs. These were stone dams built nearly
across the river but with each end open so that the fish
looking for a way through, swam through the open ends
and into another stone basin the Netsilik had built. Here
hunters would be waiting, leisters, three-pronged spears,
in hand, spearing madly at any fish they could see. There

The dog's thick coats keep
them warm and they can run
all day long, but the Eskimo
must get off and run when
the going is very rough.

The Eskimo's skilful eye
judges the correct size
of each block. Fitting
the key stone in the dome's
center is a delicate task.

was little escape for the fish. Some, who swam round the edge of the basin, might have found a small tunnel. But this too was a trap. The older men who were no longer quick enough with a leister, built these little tunnels in the stone walls, but closed up their narrowing ends. They caught the fish with their bare hands as they removed the end stone and the fish swam out. Numb with cold and wet the fishermen went back to camp when it was all over, dragging their catch on leather thongs behind them. The women gutted the trout, the men passed a fish round, and holding it very close to the mouth would slice off a piece of raw flesh to eat. Some fish were dried for later in the year. It took the women several hours to cook enough fish for the evening meal, which was eaten in two groups, the men separate from the women and children.

Before the end of August the Netsilik were again on the move, each carrying a heavy load. September was the best time for caribou hunting. For one thing they were fat after the summer grazing. Although they could be caught in spring too as they came up from the south, they were lean and their coats were too long. Autumn coats were the best for clothing, with short thick hair, each one hollow and ideal as insulation against extreme cold. As the caribou gathered in herds for their southward migration, the Netsilik intercepted them as they crossed the rivers or lakes.

But first they got out their kayaks. The frames were made of driftwood, the ribs of willow branches and they were covered with sealskin. They were hardly ever used on sea. The frames were lashed together with thongs. The hunter sat on a bearskin in the manhole.

Caribou hunting camps were built on one side of the lake preferably out of sight of the opposite shore. The Netsilik waited and watched for an approaching herd from high ground. As soon as caribou were seen approaching they made ready. Then, as they were in the water, the eldest hunter gave a signal and all started to crawl on their bellies to the water's edge. They jumped into their kayaks and paddled furiously towards the herd which was by now about half-way across and thoroughly frightened. The fastest kayakers had the best of the kill. They speared in all directions, aiming at the hindquarters or kidney regions. They killed some and wounded others, The slowest kayakers went after those who had escaped the initial onslaught. Even then some got to the far shore. But the wounded animals were not safe. They were faced with women and children, who were jumping about, waving skins in the air, screaming, shouting and imitating wolf cries. In panic the animals turned back, again to be met by the points of spears. At the end of the hunt men tied the dead caribou by their antlers to the boats, using leather thongs. If they had killed too many to bring back in this way they would wait for a favorable wind to drive the carcasses on shore.

As the igloo heats up the ice blocks melt together and the people inside stay warm even through the worst arctic gales.

Canadian Eskimo

Tired by the journey the child goes to bed under warm caribou skins. Soon the rest of the family will join him on the sleeping ledge.

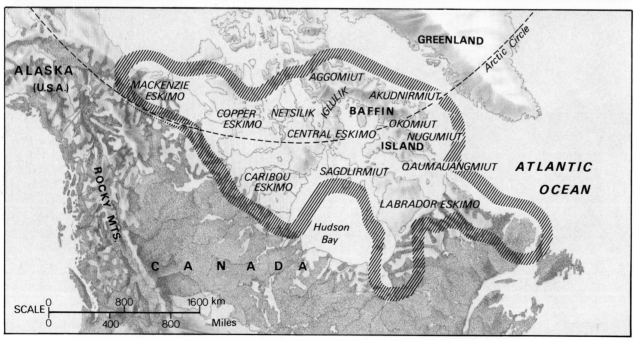

Eskimo are not always lucky
enough to have a cooking
fire. The few trees that can
stand the wind are soon
buried by snow in winter.

Chunks of raw meat lie in
the kitchen area of the
igloo. Anyone who is hungry
can cut off a piece of
frozen caribou meat.

Men butchered the animals by the shore, gulping down
the raw flesh while the children watched, waiting for the
delicacy – the eyes. On days when the caribou did not
come the children wandered about looking for Arctic
berries which ripened then. Or, they hunted seagulls
with snares. This required endless patience, one of the
most important qualities of a hunter. By early October
the lakes froze and caribou hunting ceased.

The Netsilik made their preparations for the long
winter ahead. They put up their kayaks, on big snow
mounds. The camp broke up and families went off to
look for good places for the autumn fishing before
meeting again at the sealing camps. They broke the thin
autumn ice on the lakes and took out trout, often by
using decoys. By now the seal tents were not warm
enough. The fierce autumn gales went right through
them. To keep warm the Netsilik built ice houses. They
cut ice six or seven inches thick from the rivers and
built it in blocks like an igloo, but rectangular instead of
round. They roofed this with their tent skins.

As the autumn drew to a close they began preparing
their sleds for the winter migration. Wooden sleds were
rare because of the shortage of driftwood. More often
they were made out of the old summer tents. The tent
sheets were cut in half, rolled up and each half lowered
through the ice into the river. When they were wet and

(Over page) To increase the
stamina and strength of their
dogs, Eskimo used to tie
a bitch up and leave her
to mate with wolves.

Canadian Eskimo

Inland Eskimo traditionally
live entirely on caribou meat.
Overkilling with rifles has
depleted the huge herds and
caribou is a luxury now.

Only a few caribou are killed
in winter – the stragglers
who remain while the rest of
the herd has migrated south
to the edge of the forests.

soft they were spread out. Fish were laid along one side of the tent skins. Then the two skins were rolled up very tight with the fish inside and tightly bound all around with sealskin thongs. They were left out to freeze and after being flattened with their ends turned up they formed the two runners. Caribou antlers were used for crossbars and were tied fast with sealskin thongs. A sludge of moss, snow and water was mixed together to coat the runners. It was left to freeze again before being scraped smooth with a knife or scraper. Finally it was glazed with ice. These skin runners were smooth and made travel easy.

Meanwhile the women were busy making all the winter clothes from caribou skins. Men wore pants, coats, stockings and boots, all of fur. Coats had sewn-in hoods trimmed with dog fur and long fringes. Women's clothes were alike but had larger shoulder pieces for handling babies. Babies were carried in a pouch at the back. Clothes were made of two layers. The inside layer – softer and thinner – had the fur facing the naked skin while the outside layer had the fur facing outwards. Before making the clothes the skins had to be prepared. They had to be cleaned, stretched, scraped and softened. Women did most of this work, but the men helped with the heavy scraping which was hard work. When all was ready they set off for the seals.

It was an exhausting journey and a long one. For the last month the Netsilik had been relying on stored salmon trout and caribou meat but if the season had been bad they might at this time be very hungry. Sometimes the old people could not keep up and were left behind in the snow. Very young children helped the dogs and their parents to pull the heavily laden sleds. As soon as they arrived igloos had to be built. The snow blocks were put together by men, the women heaping on loose snow to fill in the cracks and make the dwelling tight. Inside the furnishings were of snow. A sleeping counter ran round two-thirds of the wall. This was a row of snow blocks, two or three feet high with all the loose snow from the igloo floor heaped and squashed down inside. Antler ribs were put on top between the snow and the thick hair skins. A kitchen table was made for the housewife. Outside were shelters for the sleds. There was a dance house too – a larger igloo where women and children could go in the daytime, the children to play, the women to sing or dance.

The camp leader decided when and where to hunt. He was usually the oldest and most experienced hunter. He advised the keen young hunters, and encouraged the reticent and nervous. Hunters relied on their dogs' sense of smell to find the seal breathing holes for they were invisible from the surface. Sometimes they came across polar bears. These were always hunted. Vicious battles ensued and many hunters bore the scars of bear maulings.

Seals were caught most easily in the spring. By May and early June the igloos had begun to melt and had been

abandoned. Tent camps were set up on the mainland. The breathing holes were now more easily visible for the snow covering them had melted. Seals came onto the sea-ice to give birth and hunters could catch baby seals. A hunter would drag himself for hours across the wet snow on his side, feet twitching occasionally in imitation of the seal's flipper, scratching the ice with his snow knife to imitate the seal's claws and all the time crawling a few feet nearer. A good hunter would get up to twenty or even fifteen feet of a basking seal. Then he jumped up and rushed at it with his harpoon before it escaped through its breathing hole.

The Netsilik believed all humans and animals had souls. This explains many of their taboos. A freshly killed seal could not be put onto a dirty igloo floor. Fresh snow was put down. Water was poured into its mouth for it was believed the soul was still thirsty. Until it was skinned no work was done by man or woman for fear of offending the soul. And so the butchering had to be done quickly. Old blubber had to be taken out of the igloo. Caribou souls were especially delicate. While hunting caribou it was forbidden to stretch, scrape or 57

Canadian Eskimo

During a bear hunt the dogs
are released from the sled
but remain tied to one another.
As they surround the bear it
rears up to frighten them.

sew the skin. If the surrounding caribou saw what was going on they would be offended and would not allow themselves to be caught.

There were special observances too at childbirth and death. At death a human soul was supposed to live in the body for five days. At this time no-one cut their nails, combed their hair, fed their dogs, drove their sleds or cleaned their soapstone lamps. After five days the soul left the body which was then dragged out on a sled and left in the snow. Souls were believed to be transferable to babies. A woman, at delivery time, would call on the names of many souls and she often named her child after the one that was most helpful. She delivered in solitary confinement in a newly built igloo or tent and stayed there for five days. Then she was moved to another and allowed a few female visitors. Various restrictions – like not eating raw meat and only eating early in the morning and late at night – lasted a year.

Why did the Netsilik have so many taboos? For one thing their very existence hung on a thread. So much could go wrong, especially in hunting and childbirth. Misfortune could be blamed on lack of the correct taboo observances. This gave the Netsilik a tangible reason when things went wrong which they could not otherwise explain, like why children died, why animals could not be found, why there were prolonged blizzards. The

58

When the dogs have made the bear stand on its hind legs it makes an easy target for the hunter who quickly skins it after the kill.

A seal hunter shoots from the edge of the ice floe. When the seal is dead he goes out in his kayak to bring it in tied to the stern.

Breath turns to ice on modern fox fur parkas. The old parkas were edged with silky wolverine fur and breath did not freeze.

shaman could also be called upon to help put things right. In a society where there were no government officials, no very exactly defined system and no diversification of jobs, he was an important figure. He was respected for his supernatural power. He was called upon at a difficult childbirth, at unsuccessful hunts and in bad weather conditions and in quarrels between individuals. But his powers were feared as well, for he could do evil as well as good. The Netsilik spirits were not rigidly divided into good and evil ones. Good spirits could turn evil and vice versa. It was therefore important to treat them correctly.

When a girl married at about the age of 15 she simply went and began living with her husband. They were bound together by their mutual attraction and later by children whom they loved. They were also completely dependent on one another. The husband had to provide for his family while the wife had to look after the children and make all the clothes and do all the cooking. The lack of any formal marriage service made marriage no more unstable. The girl often lived with her husband's family for a little while. Relatives were recognized on both sides of the family and they supported each other. A girl was most likely to marry her first cousin as strangers were feared and distrusted.

The Netsilik also collaborated with people not of their family. Hunters shared their seal meat with those who were in no way related to them and they were bound to do this according to strict rules. The reason for this was because the family supported each other anyway, but partnership with outsiders meant that jealousies were reduced and the risk of fights decreased. No one family could always be better fed than others. The good hunters had to share their catch with the poorer ones. Most men also had song partners, men with whom they spent a lot of their time and with whom they were very friendly. Frequently song partners were so closely associated that they occasionally exchanged their wives. Wives were always consulted first but they generally agreed. But prolonged cases of wife exchange sometimes ended bitterly and dramatically with a formal end being made to the partnerships.

There was little room in Netsilik society for misfits. Every man had to be able to hunt reasonably well and he needed a wife. There were 50 recorded cases of attempted suicide in the last fifty years. In a society which numbered 260 this was a very high rate. 35 cases were successful. Sometimes a woman would kill herself if her husband was killed when hunting. As well as suicides people frequently died of starvation. In 1919 seven died near Cape Britannia and the next year sixteen men, women and children died near Simpson strait. Most suicides occurred at the beginning of the century when the Netsilik were going through a time of rapid social change. Attracted to places where there were trading posts many families emigrated and extended families

The fisherman may have to
sit by his hole all day
waiting for a bite,
so he has erected a wind
barrier for some protection.

broke up. A grown man would suddenly find that the girl who had been promised to him in marriage had disappeared and he had to find a new partner, probably a total stranger. Hunters would be using guns which meant they could kill game more easily and no longer had to depend on the support of their fellow camp members. All this meant they were more self-supporting, more dispersed, more in contact with strangers and less stable. Feelings of insecurity in the face of these changes might have also instigated some suicide cases.

Infanticide was also a response to the environment. Girls were more often abandoned than boys. For one thing they would never grow up to be hunters and contribute to the family table. If too many girls were born a mother would abandon her child. Having a child meant she had to suckle it for about two years during which time she could not have another one. By abandoning a girl child she was hopefully making room for a boy. There were several different ways of putting a child to death. In winter the infant was placed in the igloo entrance where it froze to death. It did not take very long. In summer a small stone grave was constructed near the tent and the infant was left there to die. At other times they were suffocated with furs. The biggest deterrent to infanticide was naming a child. An ancestor soul would be offended if the baby he was reincarnated in was put to death. But often this decision had been made before. Some babies were adopted once they had been abandoned. The decision to abandon a child was always made in agreement with the whole family. If a child had been promised in marriage this was also a reason for keeping it. Most cases were a direct response to outside conditions. Infanticide was the sacrifice of some individuals for the benefit of the group as a whole. One case was recorded of a couple starving on their way to Pelly bay. They were so weak they could hardly pull their sled and their eight-year old son could not walk any more. They abandoned him in the snow and went on their way.

A dog sled races across the frozen snow. For a brake the driver has nothing more than an iron spike which he pushes into the ground.

Igloolik, Caribou and Copper Eskimo

Very few white men have ever gone among the Eskimo simply to live. Some have gone into the far north in the hope of making fortunes; others have gone with a determination to change the beliefs and customs of the people they encountered there. Copper, Igloolik and Caribou Eskimo were all urged away from their traditional lives by traders and missionaries. The dates of southerners' entry into the Arctic vary from region to region. But across the Canadian north, from the Mackenzie Delta to Labrador, Eskimo have to some extent been economically, ideologically, and politically incorporated into the institutions of southern society. The process continues.

The life-style of the Copper Eskimo received its first disruption by southerners with the arrival of fur traders. They, along with missionaries, came in the wake of explorers. Diamond Jenness wrote of these changes, which even before 1920 had begun to implicate the people among whom he had lived: 'Even as we sailed away traders entered their country seeking fox-furs, always fox-furs; and for those pelts so useless for real clothing they offered rifles, shot-guns, steel tools and other goods that promised to make life easier. And so the Eskimo abandoned their communal seal hunts and scattered in isolated families along the coasts in order to trap white foxes during the winter months. Their

62

Dogs are less important in summer when the ice they sped across all winter melts and becomes the sea once again.

Fishermen push a path through 'leads' of melting ice. A skin boat can be easily crushed among the shifting ice floes.

Inukok, stone piles resembling men, stand as markers in the empty featureless wastes of the Barren lands.

(Bottom) A hunter sits perched on top of a cliff looking for whales through the telescopic sights on his rifle.

dispersal loosened the old communal ties. The men no longer labored for the entire group. Their diet and costume changed. Traders and missionaries were bent on making the Copper Eskimo into Christian trappers. Under the pressures and attractions which those newcomers wielded, the traditional way of life was unable to endure.

The Copper Eskimo were first regarded as a distinctive group by Vilhjálmur Stefánsson, who traveled among them for a year in the course of his journeys in the western Arctic just before World War I. Before Stefánsson's arrival, the Copper Eskimo were living in extraordinary isolation. Their camps were scattered along Dolphin and Union Straits, spreading north into Victoria Island and south along the Coppermine river. They were living an entirely traditional life. They had never used firearms, but hunted with bows and arrows and harpoons. Cooking pots were shaped from soft stone; heating was by seal-oil lamp. Stefánsson claims that he demonstrated the use of a rifle to Copper Eskimo hunters, but was unable to impress its effectiveness on many. They categorized it along with their shamanistic or magical techniques for hunting, which were evidently much more effective. The isolation of the group is particularly remarkable since they lived between Eskimo who had for many years been in touch with whites. But it would appear that the Copper Eskimo had a somewhat confused idea about what peoples inhabited the lands to the west and east of their own hunting grounds, whereas their western neighbors, the Mackenzie Eskimo, were themselves convinced that there were no human beings to be found in the land directly to the east of their terrain.

The date at which the Copper Eskimo spread into the regions they now occupy is not known. They speak a dialect, which is not readily comprehensible to the people who live to the west of them. It bears more resemblance to the language spoken by Eskimo to the east and south-east, but is nonetheless distinctive. Their material culture is also distinctive, principally in their use of local copper. Knife blades and other implements were traditionally made from lumps of copper which the people discovered on the open ground. The copper-rich rock was pounded into the desired shapes. No other Eskimo groups used copper or any other metal. It is from this that the Copper Eskimo receive their name.

In a multitude of other respects, however, the Copper Eskimo were much like their eastern neighbors, the Netsilik people. During winter and early spring they remained on or around the sea ice. During that time they lived off seals and polar bears. The seals are hunted at their breathing holes in the customary manner. The hunter squats or stands over the seal's breathing hole, which is concealed by snow but discovered with the help of a dog or with skilful experienced eyes. He waits for the sound of the surfacing animal's breath. The harpoon

63

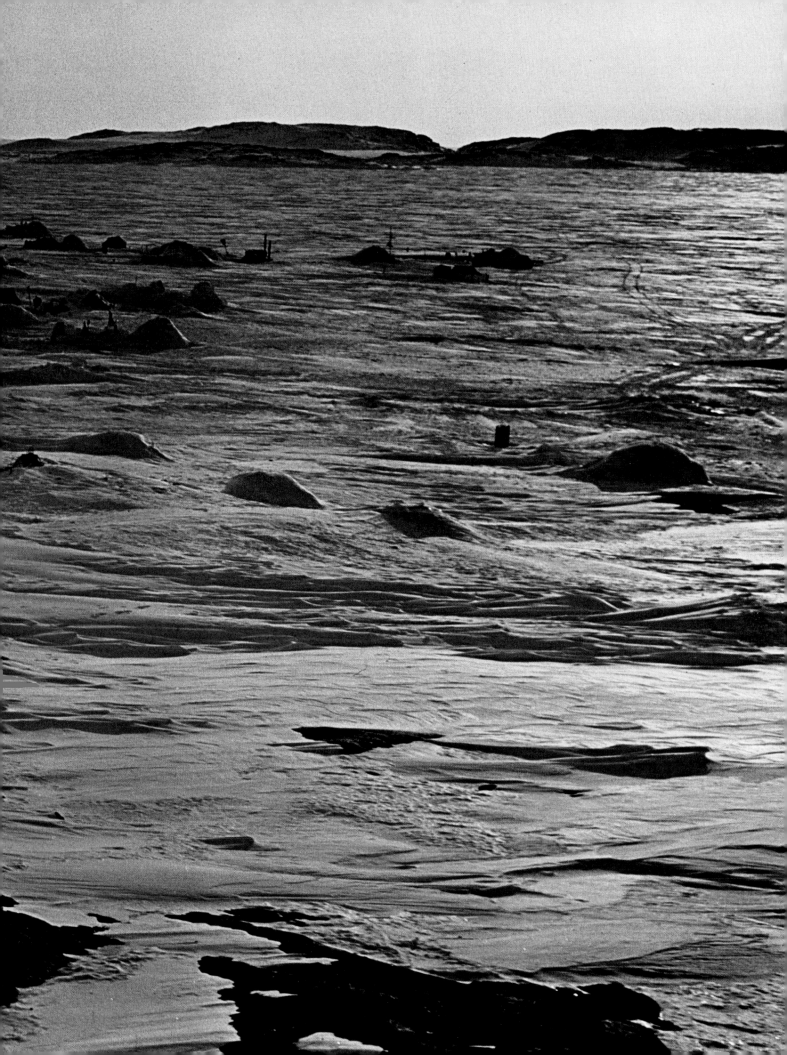

Canadian Eskimo

Children play in the tunnel
entrance to a snow house.
Igloo in Eskimo just means
'house', which can be made of
wood or skin as well as snow.

66

An Eskimo woman stands in the
traditional way, bending
straight down from the waist
as she prepares a carcass
by her canvas-roofed igloo.

There is plenty of work for a
woman during the long dark
winter. Custom forbids her
to work on skin clothes before
the first snowfall.

is the weapon, but the skill lies in timing the thrust. A hunter who stands over a breathing hole is often no more than a few feet from the head of the surfacing seal. It is essential, therefore, to keep his feet still and his weapon at the ready. It was customary for a hunter to stand facing into the wind, for then the slightest sound will be carried away from the animal. Seals surface nervously, waiting just below the surface, listening for danger. The hunter must wait until he hears the animal draw breath, and not strike at the first sound of the water lapping in the breathing hole. Only when the seal breathes can the hunter be sure that the animal's head is positioned in the space between snow cover and the surface, and only when the head is positioned is the harpoon likely to strike sure. Even when the strike is made, however, there remain difficulties. Seals are sometimes large, and it is possible that the hunter has harpooned one of the large bearded or square-flipper seals which are often more than 6 feet long. There could then follow a fierce struggle, with the hunter gripping the line tied to the harpoon blade. Traditionally a hunter looped the line around his waist and then forced it across his knees, but remained in a crouching position. In that way the strain was spread evenly, and when the seal was forced to surface to breathe the hunter would be able to club it without losing hold of his line.

All the details of seal hunting, from making the equipment to the conventions surrounding butchering the carcasses, reflect in their richness and elaboration the importance which seals occupied in traditional Eskimo

(Top) Children have no chores. Their parents say life is hard enough in the arctic, let childhood be as happy as possible.

In winter there is little to distinguish day from night and the family sleep when they are tired. Everyone huddles together under the fur robes.

Canadian Eskimo

Wooden crosses mark
the graves of settlers
at the small trading and
hunting post of Rankin
inlet on the Hudson Bay.

(Right) The midnight sun
flickers over the rooftops
of the pre-fabricated houses
built for the Eskimo by
the Canadian government.

life. Seal blubber provided heat, while the skin of the bearded seal provided the best ropes. Waterproof boots, so essential in late spring and summer were made from seal-skin. It took between five and seven seal skins to cover a kayak frame. Seal-skins made the best summer tents. It would have been hard indeed to provide sufficient skins from hunting at breathing holes. In the warmer weather of the early spring, however, the seals come out onto ice, basking and rolling in the warmth. At this time young seals are abundant. Copper Eskimo hunted seals on ice by crawling up to them, imitating the seal's movements, until it was possible to spear or even club the animals.

Once ice conditions had been transformed by the summer sun, the Copper Eskimo moved their camps inland. Caribou appear on the coast in June and July, making their way to their summer grounds. The hunters used to lie in wait for these migrating caribou at places where they would have to take to the water and where they could then be killed from kayaks. In some parts of the Copper Eskimo country deer appeared early enough in the year for it to be possible for hunters to hide in snow huts, waiting for the animals to approach so close that they could be killed with bow and arrow. Families used to travel astonishing distances during the summer months, following caribou as far as the northern edges of Victoria Island.

68

(Center) Women carry their
youngest child in an extra
pocket in the back of the
parka. There the baby stays
until the next one is born.

Skins from caribou legs
hang drying. Knee high
boots, *mukluk*, are
made from this part of
the caribou fur.

(Over page) En route to the
summer fishing ground the
wife carries the fish spear
and her husband the tent
poles and a tired child.

Two families meet on
their trek to the fishing
weir and sit down together
for a meal of dried
caribou meat.

Also during the summer families would kill fish. Cod and sculpin were sometimes taken through cracks or holes in the sea ice, but they were valuable only as a resource when sealing was proving unsuccessful. The real fishing was on lakes in the late spring. Lake trout and char were speared as they were attracted to the surface by small carved lures. The spear was a three-pronged leister, once in use throughout the Arctic. Surplus fish was sun-dried and stored. Some Copper Eskimo families spent the autumn inland, remaining close to the caribou and good fishing places, returning to the sea as late as December. Other families returned to the coast much earlier.

In general it was during winter time that large numbers of people came together; during summer they tended to scatter in very small family groups. The winter seal hunting provided the locus of most community life, and was the occasion of dancing and story-telling. Dances were usually held in a special dance house, much larger than the usual snow houses; the only instrument in use was a skin drum, and the dancer often sang a narrative song as he danced. Drumming and dancing also frequently accompanied the shamans' contact with the supernatural.

The shaman was concerned with explaining and ameliorating misfortune. Among the Copper and Caribou Eskimo shamans were many, and some were exceedingly powerful. They understood the ways in which violation of taboos brought misfortune to individuals or even to whole camps; and they could, with the assistance of special spirit helpers, make contact with the most powerful spirits. In 1923 Knud Rasmussen described a shaman's encounter with the chief spirit of the sea, Arnakapsaluk. There had been a dearth of seals, and there was hunger in a camp. It was evident that Arnakapsaluk was not allowing the seals to make their way to the surface, to their breathing holes, where the Eskimo hunters were so desperately waiting for them. The shaman called a séance, and the sea spirit spoke through him, indicting the people for 'indifference to traditions of the ancestors'. The shaman 'writhed in pain, struck out with his fists, and moaned incessantly. . . . Then, as soon as women and men had confessed all, the shaman cried in a loud voice that Arnakapsaluk's lamp was once more turned the right way up – indicating that as long as bad hunting lasted the lamp always stood bottom upwards, extinguished and dark. Shortly afterwards the shaman, who was still fighting with the Sea Woman, shouted that now her hair was smooth and clean again: for as long as all sins are not confessed her hair is usually in the wildest disorder.'

Alongside these beliefs were a multitude of stories and

myths, which gave a remarkable richness to the intellectual culture of the people. All this was intact among the Copper Eskimo during the early 1920s, although only a fragment has ever been recorded. One can but glimpse the fullness and complexity of the culture through the small pieces that have been preserved.

The Igloolik Eskimo were, in their traditional lifestyles, similar to the Copper Eskimo. But many of their camps were situated in an entirely different terrain. Spreading from the mainland adjacent to northern Foxe Basin into the northernmost edges of Baffin Island, they occupied lands which were part tundra and part dramatically glaciated coastline. To some extent the cultural difference between the Igloolik and Copper Eskimo sprang from differences in terrain. The land of Igloolik camps has always been rich in walrus and whales. The Igloolik culture is adapted to hunting and utilization of those larger mammals.

In northern Baffin Island, the narwhal pass along the coast and around the offshore islands. They appear at the floe edge in late spring, and move in large herds towards the fjords and bays as the ice breaks and scatters. Hunters were able to harpoon the narwal from kayaks, maneuvering into the herds and striking a surfacing whale with a harpoon to which was attached a large float. By following the float it was then possible to judge where the creature would next rise, and then to plunge a second harpoon *cum* float into its back. Eventually the accumulation of harpoons tired the animal, and it was possible for hunters to close on it with time to make the final kill. Floats (made from inflated sealskin) then suspended the carcass near the surface.

Able to support their large dog teams (comprizing between 15–20 dogs on harness) by their rich hauls of walrus, the Igloolik people were famous for their traveling. They appear to have ranged over enormous distances, moving from camps on the mainland of Melville peninsular to camps on Bylot Island, a distance of almost three hundred miles. Some families moved inland for the summer, walking onto the caribou grounds and spearing fish in the lakes and estuaries. But in the 19th century the arrival of whalers increased the tendency to stay all year around the coastline. Fleets of ships used to appear in summer, staying until freeze-up, or, in some cases, through the winter. These whalers were attracted by the abundance of baleen whales, and as well as using local hunters as crewmen at the shore stations they often engaged in trade – notably for walrus tusks and bear skins. The whaling was for over a hundred years extremely profitable. The price of baleen in European markets was so high that a whaling ship could cover its costs with the capture of a single whale. It was inevitable that this pursuit of fortunes would transform the life of the Igloolik Eskimo.

Those hunters, however, who remained around Foxe Basin on the western edges of the Igloolik range,

(Top) Eskimo catch char, a fish related to the salmon, as it leaves the river after spawning and makes its way back to the sea.

The char, which can reach up to 100 pounds, are gutted and laid out to dry around the skin summer tent.

73

Canadian Eskimo

In summer and autumn as much food as possible is stored or dried against the winter when hunting — and life — become precarious.

(Center) Quickly and skilfully a woman skins and cleans a seal using her *ulu*, a knife with a sharp curved copper blade.

Catching a skua, a kind of sea gull, is fun, but it is also important. Children in the Arctic learn very young how to find food.

While things are quiet in the summer camp, husband and wife make frames on which skins will be laid to dry.

avoided the whalers. The ships traveled for the most part into north Baffin along the east coast, passing westward into Eclipse Sound and around Bylot Island. Ice conditions much further north and west made whaling problematic, while the whales were most abundant in the north-eastern part of Baffin Island. To some extent the whaling divided the Igloolik culture in two, although the tendency to move back and forth across the entire culture range meant that none of the hunters was entirely isolated from southern influence. So it came about that the Igloolik Eskimo became equipped with important elements of southern material culture by the early 1800s. Guns, iron, and open whaling boats quickly came into use, while whalers' offspring were many. But these whalers did not attempt to Christianize the people they encountered, nor did they see themselves as representatives of a colonial endeavor. For the most part they were English, but they were there to get rich from whaling, not to place more territory under the British flag.

The real colonization of the Igloolik Eskimo came later, in the aftermath of the collapse of the market for baleen. That happened just prior to the World War I, when suddenly the annual arrival of ships in north Baffin came to an end. In an area less well endowed with natural resources such an abrupt change could have meant considerable hardship. In the Igloolik region it meant occasional difficulties, but there are few accounts of starvation. Moreover, in the wake of whalers came traders. In some instances they were the same people. Whalers occasionally left a ship to set up permanent trading posts. A few odd individuals had found their way into the northern end of Baffin Island by the early 1920s and were also operating as free traders. Alongside the free traders came the Hudson Bay Company, which established a post on Pond Inlet in 1927. Until a post was established at Igloolik itself the hunters and trappers of the Foxe Basin region traded their skins into Pond Inlet, some 250 miles away.

As hunters were urged to become trappers so missionaries began to move into the area. In the history of northern missions the Igloolik area is of special significance. It was the scene of a protracted struggle between Catholic and Anglican missionaries for the small Eskimo population's allegiance. Anglican and Catholic missions were established in Pond Inlet. In 1929 the Anglicans complained bitterly of 'Popery' in the area, and by 1932 the competition had become intense. Eventually it was the Anglicans who came out better in the scramble for Eskimo souls in the north Baffin region. The Catholics, however, were more successful scramblers in Foxe Basin. The communities in the area still bear scars from those disputes. In Igloolik the settlement is divided, and marriages across religious lines are still strongly discouraged by the missionaries. It is said in Pond Inlet that until recently many Eskimo believed that visiting a Catholic constituted a serious wrongdoing.

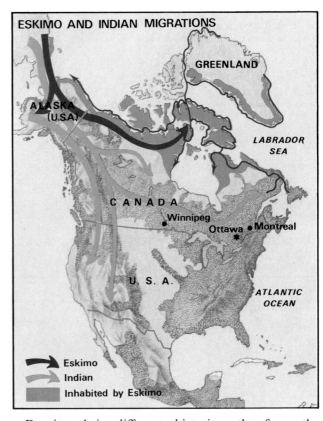

ESKIMO AND INDIAN MIGRATIONS

GREENLAND

ALASKA (U.S.A.)

LABRADOR SEA

CANADA

• Winnipeg
Ottawa • Montreal
★

U. S. A.

ATLANTIC OCEAN

➤ Eskimo
➤ Indian
▨ Inhabited by Eskimo

Despite their different histories, therefore, the Igloolik and Copper Eskimo were in much the same situation by 1940. Traditional life had given way to the fur trade, and shamans were everywhere experiencing erosion of their influence at the hands of Christianity. At the same time the locations of missions and trading posts were becoming the *loci* of established settlements. Families gathered around the new southern institutions, finding some work there and inclining towards an altogether more settled life. But the majority of families throughout the Igloolik culture remained in camps, trapping and hunting. Thus the transition from traditional subsistence to living by the fur trade was effected.

The Caribou Eskimo were much more directly vulnerable to change in their traditional life than either the Copper or Igloolik people. They were the only Canadian Eskimo who did not depend in substantial measure upon sea mammals. They lived inland, west of Hudson Bay, from northern Manitoba to around Baker lake in the North-West Territories. The basis of their subsistence was the caribou, which passed through their lands in massive numbers on their migrations north in the spring and south in the autumn. The Caribou Eskimo hunted these animals along the migration routes. A favored method of hunting was by way of an avenue of cairns, along which hunters were hidden. These 'avenues' alarmed the herds, which forced them to keep to their center. But since the distance between the cairns 75

The profit from the summer catch of seal skins will see the Eskimo family through the winter when hunting is poor and game scarce.

(Bottom) *Ulu*, made of raw beaten copper have bone handles. The woman's *ulu* has a curved blade for scraping skins clean.

gradually narrowed, the animals eventually came within range of the hidden archers. Another method involved the use of sticks festooned with bird wings or scraps of skin. These sticks created the appearance of movement, and were doubly alarming to the herds which were easily driven between them towards a place where they were more easily approached – typically to a river or lake which animals would attempt to cross. Once a large number of caribou had taken to the water, hunters would be able to go among them in their kayaks, spearing them in large numbers. Other techniques included pitfalls and artificial trails which herds were inclined to follow, and beside which hunters could hide.

The Caribou Eskimo made all their clothes from scraped caribou hides, and used hides for their tents as well. Since the southern edges of their range lay within the tree line, wood could be used for fuel. Further north tents and snow houses could only be heated with tallow candles, which burned caribou fat. But such fat as was available constituted an important part of the people's diet, while caribou tallow is an entirely inadequate lamp fuel compared with sea mammal blubber. So many Caribou Eskimo spent much of the winter in unheated snow houses. This was possible only because their caribou skin clothing was of remarkable quality. Yet Caribou skin clothing remains efficient only so long as conditions are perfectly dry. In winter it was dry while the snow houses remained cold. In spring, or when a snow house became humid, the skin clothing quickly soaked and lost its insulation.

The highly specialized nature of the Caribou Eskimo culture with its apparent material poverty, has led many observers to regard them as the hardiest people in the world. The barren lands are intensely cold during winter, and there is no doubt that the Caribou Eskimo suffered recurrent privations when the migrating herds failed to appear, or appeared later than usual. But in the past caribou were abundant. The direst circumstances arose with the appearance of the gun and the decline in caribou population after traders and others had begun to deplete the herds. Caribou Eskimo utilized the fish and bird resources of their country, but they never developed nets. During the winter the birds in any case disappeared from their land. It was not possible for them to survive the long winters without stocks of caribou.

They lived in remarkable isolation. Exploration of the Canadian Arctic proceeded for the most part by sea routes; although Samuel Hearne passed directly across the Caribou Eskimo hunting grounds in the late 18th century he apparently saw none of the Eskimo hunters. In the 1850s John Richardson, a distinguished Arctic explorer, was convinced that no Eskimo lived inland. It was J B Tyrrell who first realized that the Barrens were inhabited by caribou-hunting Eskimo – and that was only in 1895. It thus happened that the time of the Caribou Eskimo's discovery was also the time of their

A tangle of caribou
antlers outside the tent is a
source of pride — it shows that
the man inside is a good hunter
with a well fed family.

worst starvations. They were studied between 1920 and 1950 by a series of distinguished ethnographers, who leave a record of the desperate condition of these people. It is almost certain that the Caribou Eskimo suffered radical depopulation from recurrent starvation throughout that period. By the 1940s very few remained on the land. Attention was drawn to their situation by Farley Mowat, who spent time among them in 1947 and 1948. Between 1949 and 1951 the people he had known were struck with starvation and disease. Mowat has argued that the deficiency in the people's diet which resulted from caribou population decline severely reduced their resistance to those infectious diseases which white presence in the far north had spread among the Eskimo people.

Although the Eskimo themselves lived in isolation, the caribou upon which they depended did not. They were hunted all along their migration routes. Chipewyan Indians had always hunted them in the south, only slightly beyond the range of the Caribou Eskimo. To the north were the Netsilik, Aivilik, and Igloolik Eskimo, who were partly dependent on the herds. But with the advent of firearms, depletion of the stock was drastic

Eskimo suffered tragically from
their early contact with white
men — polio, 'flu, tuberculosis
decimated whole tribes. Babies
born now are much healthier.

(Over page) Forced by nature
to adapt to the land, Eskimo
especially the children,
are now learning to adapt
to the white man's world.

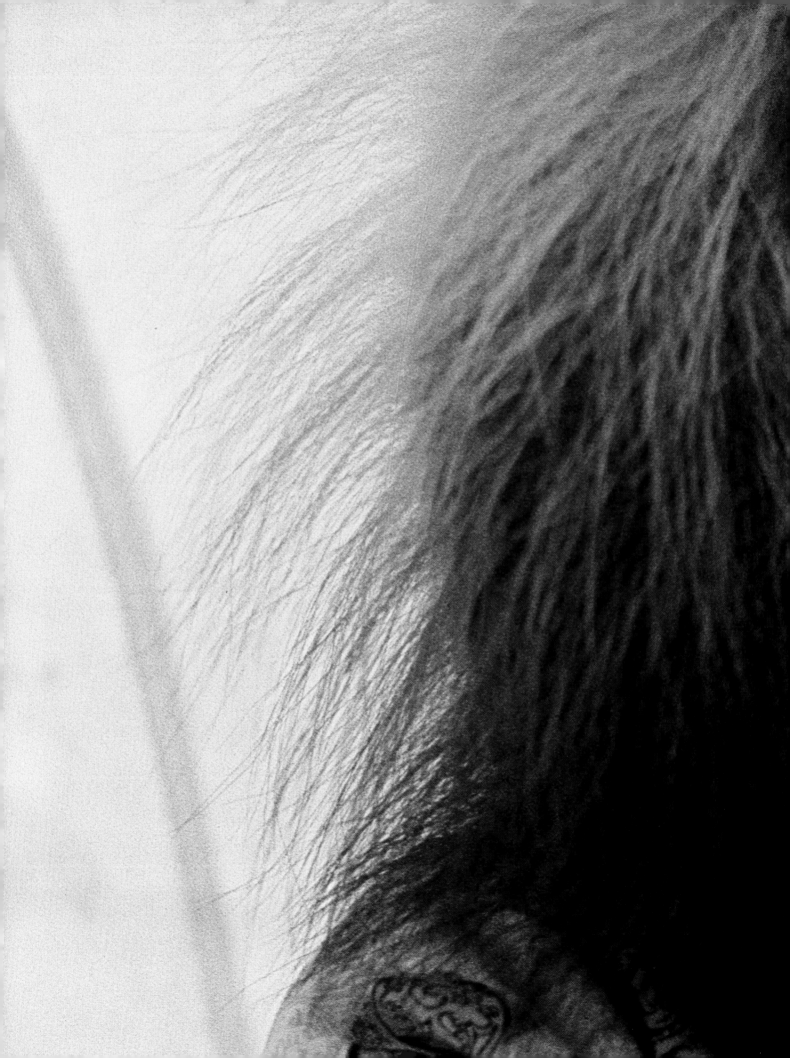

The time has come to leave
the summer camp and start the
trek back to the village.
The husband helps his wife
adjust her load.

at every point, while at the furthest edge of the southern migration, in the wintering grounds among the trees, white trappers, traders and adventurers were also predating on the vulnerable animals. Along the line were the Caribou Eskimo, who were the most dependent on caribou, and much the least able to accommodate to their decline. They became victims of changes in the north before the men creating the changes knew anything of their existence.

To some extent it was the fate of the Caribou Eskimo which highlighted a multitude of new changes in the Canadian north, changes which have significantly revised the life-styles of the Igloolik, Copper, and all other Eskimo. After World War II the Canadian government assumed a much more direct responsibility for the original northern people. The fur trade had begun to collapse at the beginning of the war, and fur prices continued to hover around low levels in the decade following the war. Those hunters who had turned into trappers of the white fox were thus obliged to suffer the consequences of shifts in the world fur market. Just at the period when they had become critically dependent upon the goods which were exchangeable for fox skins, the skins fell drastically in value. To get sufficient goods became extremely hard. Without those goods many camps throughout the Arctic were threatened with dangerous shortages of what had become vital supplies. At the same time the Canadian Federal Government became anxious about extending medical and educational facilities to the

remoter parts of the north, and were also concerned with establishing an administrative framework within which the northern peoples would have a definite place.

Special impetus was given to these national concerns by the state of Eskimo health. The facts which began to receive publicity in the 1950s were indeed alarming. During 1948-9 an epidemic of poliomyelitis broke out among Eskimo living along west Hudson Bay, including some of the Caribou Eskimo camps: 18 adults died, and 60 were paralyzed (representing just under 8 per cent of total population). In some camps the incidence of infection was close to 100 per cent. In early 1952 southern Baffin was the scene of a serious measles epidemic during which the mortality rate in three communities rose to 22 per cent. During the measles epidemic there was a concurrent outbreak of influenza 'B' and that epidemic was followed by the spread of scarlet fever and mumps. Throughout the Arctic these epidemics spread debilitation and a corresponding dependence upon southern agencies. But the most troubling, and most pernicious of the widespread disease of that period, was of course tuberculosis. It was discovered in the early 1960s, for example, that 55 per cent of all households in Baker Lake contained at least one case of tuberculosis, and that one half of all the children in that community were actively infected. In 1954 an article appeared which revealed that the tuberculosis rate among Indians and Eskimo was between 15 and 20 times higher than the Canadian national rate. It was also pointed out that the

80

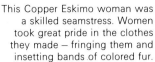

Belongings are piled high for
protection from scavengers and
to keep them above the snow
until the owners return with
dog sleds for the heavy load.

This Copper Eskimo woman was
a skilled seamstress. Women
took great pride in the clothes
they made — fringing them and
insetting bands of colored fur.

birthrate was double, whereas the infant mortality rate was three times as high.

During the 1950s and early 1960s medical ships made annual visits to the shore camps of many northern Eskimo. In this way the Igloolik and Copper Eskimo received some medical help. But since summer was a time when many families traditionally were pursuing the caribou inland, even that small service illustrates how southern attention was almost invariably disruptive. The people, however, were in no mood to resist such disruptions; they had become direly in need of southern support. It was in that mood that many families moved from their camps to larger, permanent settlements. At first some families remained in camps, while their children were taken to school in the settlements. In Pond Inlet, for example, there was a large hostel for the children of those families who wished to stay on the land as trappers. But for many parents, living without their children was insufferable, and they gradually moved to the settlements too. Families were encouraged to leave those areas where game resources did not appear sufficient. Many Caribou Eskimo were urged to move from their inland camp sites to work at a mine being developed during the 1960s at Rankin Inlet on the Hudson Bay shore. Others were lured into Baker lake, which rapidly grew into a sizeable village. Most of the Copper Eskimo moved into Holman and Coppermine.

The hunters and trappers came to abandon their camps. In 1971 there were still two camps in north Baffin,

and two others in northern Foxe Basin, but by 1972 they had also been abandoned. By 1970 there were none left among the Caribou Eskimo, and none among the Copper Eskimo. Some men still hunted and trapped, and some families went camping for as much as two months in the spring. But they had established their homes in the settlements. The Canadian government had initiated a comprehensive housing program, whereby every family was supplied with a southern-style low rental home. The houses have oil fired heating, one or two bedrooms, and are equipped with basic furnishings. They are prefabricated, and shipped in sections to the settlements during the summer. They have become one of the hallmarks of modern Eskimo living. Lacking bathrooms and often poorly constructed, their outward appearance soon comes to represent the cultural changes occurring inside. Many hunters and trappers are becoming poor members of Canadian society. New problems revolve round overcrowding, shortage of money, inadequate job opportunities.

The settlements in which Igloolik, Copper and Caribou Eskimo live today vary in size from 200 to 500 people. They have a dual society, of Eskimo and whites. The social gulf between southerners and the Eskimo they teach and administer is vast: they rarely visit one another, and when they do, seem to find the experience embarrassing. Differences in social attitude add to language barriers. Whites and Eskimo who seek occasionally to communicate, talk across cultural distances 81

Canadian Eskimo

Caribou have not been hunted with bow and arrow for many years. When traders brought rifles, the Eskimo forgot how to make the old weapons.

Igloos are inadequate against the Arctic climate. The Eskimo's real protection from the cold is the double layer of fur clothing.

and in spite of awkward preconceptions about one another. Yet settlement life is the mainspring of rapid change. Whatever adaptations the Eskimo make to change will occur in the everyday affairs of those uneasy villages. Economically the settlement gives some degree of support. There are jobs to be had driving trucks, organizing basic services, making and maintaining roads, assembling the prefabricated house sections. Many young men are being trained as heavy equipment operators and mechanics. The hope is that future development of Canada's north will provide wage employment for all who seek it. In north Baffin the development of the Arctic islands oil and gas industry has created some 24 jobs for young men prepared to work for 20 days in each month on the 7 drilling sites. It is there that the rush of change receives its most poignant expression. Among the site workers are men who were born and raised in remote high Arctic camps, who have learned to be skilled hunters, who lived on the land, following the caribou in summer and hunting the sea mammals during winter. Some of those men came to settlement life from camps only five years ago, with some reluctance, proud of their skills as hunters and troubled by the 'crowded' life in a village of three hundred people. At those oil and gas exploration sites the men shovel mud or operate trucks. They earn slightly less than $10 000 per annum.

The future of the Canadian Arctic is not clear. It may be that large-scale economic development will reform the landscape and the economic lives of the people who once lived and traveled so skilfully there. It may happen, however, that the people of the Copper, Igloolik and Caribou cultures will become a small part of the labor resources which that development will need. If so, it is likely they will be considered unqualified for skilled work and unentitled to ownership or control. If so, their

So that the bone frame of a kayak or sled could be securely lashed with hide thongs, it was first pierced with a bow-drill like this one.

lands may be developed by outsiders for outsiders. Some of the Canadian Eskimo are beginning to express anxiety about such possibilities, and are undertaking a campaign aimed at resisting, or at least limiting, such southern exploitation of the land. Even those men who have regular jobs remain preoccupied with the land. All Eskimo still like to hunt. When an oil company returns a work crew to a settlement after a 20 day shift, even those highly paid laborers prefer to spend much of their 10-day break hunting. While those with highly paid regular work remain a minority, many families still depend on what all families prefer – the 'real, wild food' which the hunters bring home.

All the settlements now have community councils, elected locally, and charged with some limited responsibility for settlement affairs. But their political power is small. There is an ongoing attempt to increase the influence of local councils, and to bring local Eskimo politics in line with local government practices in the rest of the country. But those political institutions tend to be hollow. The most important matters remain under the control of the nation's larger institutions, while many Eskimo are alarmed at the changes engulfing them. Those who wish to be hunters and trappers are faced with economic difficulties. Those who want to be wage-laborers are vulnerable to southern agencies. Yet the Eskimo do not see how they could chart a course of their own through these fundamental difficulties. Responsibility for real change lies far beyond their political compass.

Finally, the problems for settlement Eskimo are essentially uniform, and the policies which governments design for meeting those problems apply throughout the Canadian north. The traditional life was ethnographically complex. There were real differences in the ways the cultures had refined their techniques and their intellectual life. Their clothing styles were different, their kayaks were different, and they held different versions of a broadly similar cosmology. Today Igloolik Eskimo of the settlements laugh at the bizarre manner in which Caribou Eskimo talk – and *vice versa*. And there remains a consciousness of styles of dress. But those variations sprang from social and economic contexts which have almost all been eclipsed by modernizations and the spread of southern concerns. Today the Copper, Igloolik and Caribou Eskimo have in common the matter of jointly dealing with the newest and largest forces which threaten to engulf them entirely. The details of their separate cultures have become a matter of ethnographic reconstruction; the future of the Canadian Eskimo as a whole is uncertain and troubling, a matter of speculation. That future will be determined by economic and social forces which are far indeed from the caribou, seals, narwhal and the limitless tundra over which the cultures developed their intricacies and separate excellence.

83

Baffin Island Eskimo

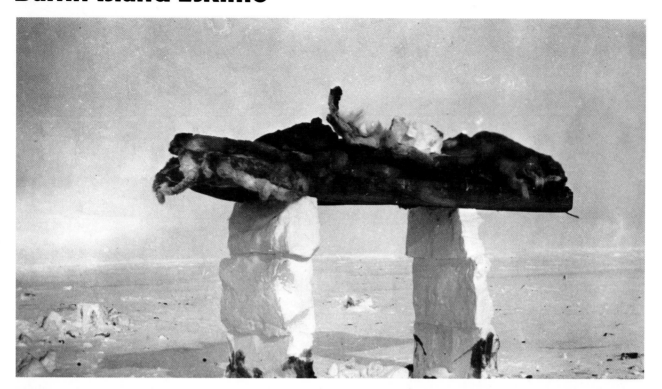

Until the 1950s the Canadian government interest in the Baffin islanders was mainly confined to occasional police patrols. But recently the majority of the once nomadic Baffin islanders have come together in fixed settlements which the Canadian government has supplied with prefabricated houses, health, educational, social welfare and development services. In Frobisher Bay is the largest settlement, 1,000 strong. Many Eskimo are employed to provide services for 600 Canadian residents. The remaining 2,500 Eskimo live scattered in seven other coastal settlements.

The Eskimo depended on animal skin and bone for clothing, utensils and hunting implements. The back sinews of caribou were used for thread; seal blubber was used for fuel. They ate the bulk of their food raw. Effective clothing was important in an environment where the winter temperature often drops below −30°F. Jackets, pants, mitts and boots were made of double layers of caribou skin, the hair on the inner layer turned inwards to trap the body warmth, and that on the outer layer turned outwards. But caribou skin is not waterproof and during the time of melting snow and ice in spring and summer they used scraped seal skin. They used stone and wood too. They quarried soapstone which is soft and easily hollowed into blubber-burning lamps and cooking pots. Since Baffin Island is entirely tundra, wood was less easy to find, though they needed it for harpoon shafts, sled runners and for boat frames. Driftwood was found on the island shores and some came from the Eskimo in Quebec who traded across the

84

(Top) A cache at a sealing camp in Franklin Bay is the same as the caches the Eskimo have always made each autumn to secure a winter food supply.

Wrapped in a caribou skin shroud the corpse of a Netsilik Eskimo lies above the permanently frozen soil on King William island.

A Netsilik hunter wears
driftwood 'goggles'
to protect his eyes from
the glare of light
reflected from the ice.

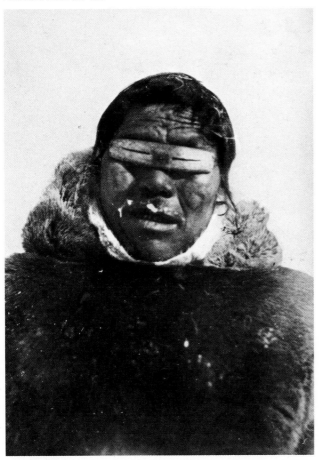

Hudson Bay, and who lived near the tree line.

Summer was the most comfortable time of year. Small groups of three or four families lived inland, fishing at stone weirs and then stalking caribou with bows and arrows. Sometimes larger groups of Eskimo were attracted by large herds of caribou. Women and children would try to deflect them through alleys of stone cairns while hidden archers would be waiting at the end. Before the sea froze round the shores in October, the Baffin islanders would hunt on the coast, harpooning seals from kayaks and stalking walruses that had hauled themselves onto rocky islets. The Eskimo had to store much of the meat for the approaching winter, the harshest time of year. Then they clustered for security in groups, several hundred strong. When possible they went with dogs and harpoons to search the ice for seals' breathing holes over which they would wait motionless in bitter conditions for a seal to come and breathe.

Or, if the ice edge was close to shore, the hunters might look for seals and walruses in the open water beyond. If food was plentiful, the many winter days of confinement, blizzard-bound to igloos, were times for recreation in large community igloos. But starvation was not uncommon in winter. A neighboring camp 100 miles away was too distant to help, and legends tell of occasions when dogs and even human bodies were eaten. Only in the warmer days of spring would winter groups, the largest of the year, split up as hunting became less hazardous. The Eskimo remained on the sea ice until the end of June when it broke. This nomadic cycle and the social organization it involved reflected the availability of various types of game and the rigors of Arctic life.

The virtual absence in Baffin Island of female infanticide indicated that the environment was not particularly severe. It was a practice common among Eskimo groups to the west who lived in harsher conditions and which ensured that proportionately larger numbers of children grew to be men, the providers of, rather than dependents on, the family food supply. However, like Eskimo everywhere, the Baffin islanders had to cope with the luck and the risks of hunting. The kinship ties that joined the members of their groups guaranteed that the fortunate supported the less lucky. Eskimo who were unrelated regarded each other with suspicion as potential enemies. Baffin islanders had no fixed leaders. Men of personality and hunting ability would have influence so long as they could demonstrate their superiority by supporting larger numbers of dogs, wives (seldom more than two) and poorer dependents, than other Eskimo.

The arrival of American and European whalers a hundred years ago particularly affected the Eskimo in the south-east of the island where whalers operated shore stations and occasionally billeted their crews with Eskimo families. Although the rifles which the Europeans traded improved Eskimo hunting, the diseases they also brought decimated the population. In a few decades Eskimo numbers dropped from about two thousand to little more than one thousand. Having almost exterminated the whale the whalers withdrew. They were replaced by traders who sought to persuade the Eskimo to trap animals for furs, particularly the white fox. With hunting now easier, the Eskimo could rear larger dog teams – of a dozen or more animals – and travel more easily to their inland trapping grounds in winter. During the fur trade boom of the 1920s the most successful trappers bought 40-foot powered fishing boats, enlisted kinsmen as their crew and organized summer expeditions to hunt seals and walruses for winter supplies.

Fox prices slumped in the 1930s depression and the islanders found it difficult to purchase the European equipment on which they had come to depend. But unlike other regions of Arctic Canada, Baffin Island did not suffer the drastic reductions in the caribou population that caused widespread starvation among other Eskimo peoples. During such hard times, the Eskimo could no longer seek the comfort of their shamans, for these had been discredited by Anglican and Catholic missionaries who had also admonished the Eskimo for practising polygamy, infanticide and for exchanging wives, the traditional gesture of friendship between men.

Polar Eskimo
northern Greenland

The Polar Eskimo live further
north than anyone else in
the world. In north-west
Greenland a group sets off on
a seal hunting expedition.

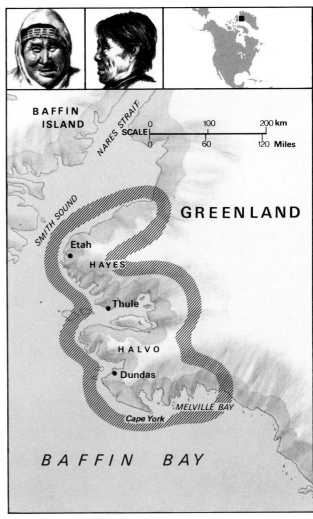

The Polar Eskimo are the most northerly-dwelling human society of our planet. Known since the beginning of our era, and doubtless older than that – about 3,000 to 4,000 years – they live in the north-west of Greenland from 76°50′ to 80°N in the district of Thule. They are geographically isolated by Melville Bay in the south, which is uninhabitable for lack of ice-free ground, and by Ellesmere Land, which has remained uninhabited since the middle ages.

At the threshold of the glacial ocean the Polar Eskimo, who have oscillated in numbers between being 150-strong as they were at the time of their discovery in 1818 and 500-strong in 1973, represent a true example of an Eskimo society which lives in a state of wise equilibrium between its needs and its resources. The expeditions of Knud Rasmussen in 1922–25 which founded contemporary eskimology were assured by the generosity of the Thule Trading Post. In the same way all the coastal Eskimo cultures of Canada, Alaska and Siberia which are similar to those of Thule have, with reference 87

Polar Eskimo northern Greenland

to their benefactors, been called 'Thule cultures'.

Eponymous Thule. Thule which borders on the Magnetic Gulf and is at the very center of the Northern Lights. Thule the crossroads of the routes of all the American migrations which culminated in the peopling of Greenland. Thule the support, with Peary and Cook, of American polar enterprises. Thule the seat of the Arctic military base which is the most powerful in all the western hemisphere. Thule, finally, which since time immemorial has been the territory of among the richest and best preserved populations of fox and seal-hunters in all the Arctic. Such are some outstanding characteristics concealed in this prestigious Faustian name.

It was on 9 August 1818 that the 150 Polar Eskimo of Thule were discovered by the west. John Ross on board the *Isabella and Alexander* was searching for the Franklin expedition. By chance he saw on the desolate shores some 'human animals' which William Baffin had been too distracted to spot when he made his voyage of discovery in 1600. The closest of all human populations to the Pole entered history.

These people's destitution was extreme. A cold era – the little ice age – which began in 1600 was drawing to a close. Under the instructions of their shamans – or *angakoks* – the Eskimo had confronted this with self-restraint. They imposed voluntary restrictions on themselves, prohibitions on sexual, eating and hunting activities. These sacrifices, which were so harsh for a group of 50 to 80 hunters, isolated like lost children, cannot be understood except against the background of permanent planning which rules their lives.

88

Inflated sealskins float like buoys. Harpoons are attached to them so they cannot be lost if the hunter misses his mark.

The hunter missed but he has collected his harpoon from the *avataq* or blown up sealskin, used only for open sea fishing.

(Bottom) A seal, whose flesh is eaten and whose chewed pelt will be used for clothing and kayak skins, is dragged ashore – often with ropes of sealskin.

hues of the ground, the paths followed by the hares and foxes. All along the shoreline they assess the density of the birds' flight-formations, which indicate the presence of shoals of little fish and are a future guarantee of numerous seals and walruses. They discuss the movements and changes of habit of fauna, indeed everything which reflects the entire ecology. They have detailed knowledge of the morphology, osteology, diets and ethology of all the animals that live around them. These men become aware of, and then exchange, an accumulation of thousands of signs. All these indications enable the group to decide, in consensus and in good time, the proper course of action to adopt.

In August 1818 the Thule Eskimo responded with fear to the interrogations of the grandly uniformed English officers. Through an interpreter the newcomer learned that these men believed that they were the only men in the world and that according to an old belief, they were awaiting the arrival of men from the south who would come in boats equipped with great wings. Their poverty was evident. There were just one to two dogs for each sledge. They lacked driftwood and their sledges and tools were formed out of little seal and walrus bones. Their clothes were of dog, seal or bearskin. Their sole source

This planning requires that the Eskimo exactly proportion their resources to their needs, certainly. But above all it means advance planning. Eskimo women in effect have children only once every 28 months. The espectation of life is low: 22 for women and 27 for men in 1951. And infant mortality is high: two out of three children die. These planning systems are twofold. Periods of temperate climate are met with a system of shoreline whale hunting, caribou hunting and salmon fishing. And cold periods are countered with temperance, with if not dietary restrictions (only birds killed in summer are eaten all year round) at least sexual restrictions (involving various taboos concerning only the men) and even population restrictions: two out of three baby girls are killed at birth.

The decisions are made. They take into account assessments of the climate which these men of nature can make two or three years in advance. Hunters who draw life's essentials from the ice-bank they follow and minutely examine the flight of migratory birds, the slightest nuances of the seasons to come, the thaws of the ice on sea and land, the direction of the drifts, the relative movements of shoreline and sea, the depth here, and there, of the thaw, the mutations and changes in the

89

A dead walrus lies as evidence of this hunter's skill with a harpoon. The sealskin float has marked the kill.

Polar Eskimo northern Greenland

Aim is taken through a hide, the seal unaware of his danger. In the past the Eskimo got close to seals by imitating them.

(Bottom) A long trench is cut in the ice, through which a net is lowered to trap fish swimming across it by the gills.

Famished huskies — the hunter's allies — are tossed some lumps of seal meat. In the hunting season they get fed every second day.

of minerals was three meteorites from which they would knock off little pieces to make harpoon points and various kinds of knife. Their igloos were of stone interspersed with turf. Even in the very worst famines they ate neither the profusion of reindeer meat, nor salmon. They were ignorant of the kayak and of the bow which their great ancestors had known and used before the little ice age. They had come to forget certain descriptive names – *Toukto* the reindeer for example – even though these animals, objects and practices were profoundly rooted in their memories.

The careful study of the demographic structure of this tribe and of its evolution in time indicated that the situation of this population, which grows at a feeble annual rate of 0.8 per cent, has always been precarious. The Polar Eskimo have a faculty – remarkable among a rigorously isolated low-strength group, which was without doubt the case from 1600 to 1901 and most certainly true from 1818 to 1860 – of subjugating their demography by forbidding all consanguinious marriage. This accords with a rough planning system. It would appear from my researches that all unions with cousins up to the sixth degree have been avoided. Equal consideration must be given to the prohibition on all sexual contact between married couples during periods of mourning for close relatives, infanticide of baby girls at birth in times of hardship and the exchange of wives to encourage maximum fecundity. But can these various prohibitions really account for the mechanisms by which the group increases or reduces its demographic consistency? With such relatively narrow margins it is without doubt possible to reply in the affirmative.

But how can one explain the demographic bulge in the 1860–1895 period? Let us briefly recall the facts. In 1855–1860 the group was undergoing great difficulties. It had just experienced, in succession, a prolonged period of intensified cold and a terrible famine. The Eskimo then had no more than 32 women capable of procreating. These 32 procreant women of 1855–1860 (even if we assume that no infanticide intervened) could only engender a total of 16 up to 1872, among whom would number 16 per cent cases of sterility (as was characteristic of Eskimo in 1950). In other words these 32 women could produce only 14 individuals capable of reproduction. And if the period of fertility had not exceeded 12 years five months the women capable of being mothers in 1860 would in 1872 have become sterile, even before the four women born in 1863 would be

A team of dogs and men haul a seal back to camp across the ice floes, where it will be scrupulously divided among camp members.

(Over page) A skin tent set on the shore is witness to the unforgiving vastness of northern Greenland, where the sun never rises for four months.

91

Polar Eskimo northern Greenland

The bearskin pants
worn by Polar Eskimo are
unique. In 1818 there
were 150 Eskimo there
but now there are 500.

capable of reproduction. Certainly the nine little girls born in 1860 – reduced by the average sterility rate to seven – could 'deliver the goods'. But what expectations can one have of a society whose entire fate depends on just seven women? In fact, supposing that, for the period under consideration, there was a total proscription on infanticide, that all the matrimonial and genetic rules and prohibitions had been suspended, the average rates of fertility, sterility and inbreeding characteristic of the group will necessarily limit the annual maximum level of demographic growth of 0.8 per cent.

Now this rate, between 1860 and 1895 turns out to be nearly 300 per cent higher.

At a time when the climate warms up, as was the case, even the alternative levers of genetic liberty and genetic regulation and of the practice or the proscription of infanticide – which the Eskimo so wisely understood – are not enough to explain this 300 per cent increase.

In these small, very specific human groups, who have for hundreds of generations suffered considerable physical constraints in isolation, we are forced to admit that there are some fundamental mutations. These mutations must have affected their characteristics of fertility, genetic longevity and of interbreeding – indeed of natural masculinity itself.

A biological privilege? In our latitudes, as must be the

case in Thule, there are in the area of immunology numerous examples of phenomena of organic intelligence. And here we have a quite new field of research.

Thule society represents a little more than one per cent of the Greenland population. Now it draws for itself alone on more than 12 per cent of the entire island's products of hunting. Here we speak of its wealth. The migratory birds – some millions of auks – are the reason for the country's abundance of foxes and seals.

Just over 70 hunters. That is the size of society which supplies goods to the value of 25,000 dollars per year. But in return this same society only disposes of an effective revenue of a little under 1 dollar per month per head. And from this must be deducted the financing, the depreciation of capital goods (crossbars, sledges, guns, cartridges . . .) and all the general expenses of production.

This invested amount which yields 28 times its value, would without doubt be one of the most profitable in the world. Now the Polar Eskimo receives a little less than one-fifth of the wealth which he produces.

Social life, economic life and daily life proceed from the most precise psychological data, from characteristics of the indigenous mentality, the cultural categories by which the Eskimo informs his perception of the world in which he lives and acts.

This perception rests first and foremost on principles

94

of inequality. Inequality of ages first. A boy who is too young to marry or who has no allocated task is not authorized to take part in debates. He stands, propping up the door of the igloo where the men are assembled. He participates, falsely expressionless, in silence. One can observe the same of the old man, living apart in his tent or igloo, who would once have been abandoned in times of hardship. The big options are the prerogative of the producers. The young, the old and the women resemble nothing so much as a classical Greek chorus.

There are the strong. And there are the weak, the incapable. The latter justify their presence by making a whole gamut of silent and servile compensatory gestures: a way of walking, a way of carrying themselves, a tone of voice reveal the order of things. The scorn of the strong for the weak is sometimes so great that it is translated into acts of violence. At Hudson Bay in Igloolik in 1961 it fell to me to witness a 'parasite' slaughtered by his adversary after a fight. To better demonstrate his strength and superiority the victor urinated on his victim.

Finally there is the awareness of regional inequalities. The vast district constitutes a source of wealth by its very diversity. The group lives in a territory made up of five complementary subdivisions and it is by family alliances substantiated by exchanges of surplus goods that the group defines its unity. Each family installs itself for two or three years in each section of the district. During the course of a continuous rotation from north to south the head of the family exchanges his house of stone with this or that person; the hunting areas are tribal property and the house is a 'commune bonum'. Thus families cannot be regionalized and political appropriation is impossible. And the tribe remains one.

Essential fact: neither the young Eskimo nor the woman, nor the bad hunter, nor the man without kin, nor the weak, nor the Eskimo who is a recent immigrant, nor the Eskimo installed because of family connection in a bad hunting area has contested – nor do they now contest – the legitimacy of the discrimination inflicted on them. The social structure is appropriate to the place they live in and not to the men who live in it. The law and values of the group take precedence over those of the individual.

However varying and plastic the group may appear it in fact has a hard interior core. It has an ordered structure. More than a collection of individuals or an accumulation of groups, it is a tool, an assembly of means of survival informed by more than a thousand years of perils. One authority interprets these.

In Foxe Bay in Canada this authority is called *issoumater*. *Issouma*: thought. *Issoumatar*: the man who thinks a lot, the wise man. At Thule they have the *nalagaq*, implying more authority than wisdom.

The *nalagaq* or *issoumatar* is an adroit hunter. He is the man who, by his authority and by his spirit of fore-

sight and organization, assures the group's resources.

The *issoumatar* must, more than any other man, be modest, calm, humorous and quiet. He represents that type of mysteriously strong personality that the group, luck and the elements elect. The chosen *issoumatar* is unceasingly constrained to surpass himself. He is irrevocably committed, inextricably involved. He understands that even in the eyes of his own people, his gifts and functions must be counterweighed and guaranteed by great enterprises and great successes.

Physical strength and superiority. The group's entire standard of living depends in effect on these qualities. But abundance and ease would be pointless if the leader's intrinsic qualities did not also assure internal peace of the group. And if by safeguarding its social cohesion he did not double the chances of its physical survival. Not only the *issoumatar's* generosity, the egalitarian character of the sharing out of the takings makes any individual hoarding and differentiation by wealth impossible. To him the prestige and authority. To each man, and in equal parts, the benefits.

A great past, prestigious ancestors, a shamanistic line, an innate gift of authority and wisdom, of pride, gaiety,

An Eskimo drinks thirstily from melted snow on an icefloe. Sea ice can be used for drinking since long freezing diminishes the salt content.

95

of luck, a deep rooting in the country, those are the conditions. The designation of such a leader is in fact the effect of a natural necessity and a spontaneous act.

From July 1952 a US military base of about 5,000 people was set up at Thule. It represented a dramatic confrontation between the two societies – the one traditional and directed towards the exploitation of natural resources, the other military, parachuted from the south.

Maintaining their history and passing on their heritage intact were for 2,000 years the principal motivations of the Eskimo's quixotic combat. And nowhere is there anything more ancient and more respectable than this millenarian instinct.

Everything in this 20th century invites the man of the extreme north to renunciation and to acquiescence. And contrary to what his pride would have him believe, time is not in his favor.

The internationalization of culture is for ever more rapid on our planet. Here we must speak of the customary processes by which an archaic society begins to acquire the vices of the dominant society. This society in its weakened state decides to imitate the dominant society in its virtues which, in the state of decadence in which it has fallen, are deadly to its own spirit.

When it comes to hunting – and this is everybody's business at Thule, for there are no other prospects – the essential problem is a problem of price and payment.

The question arises as follows: should one first help a society which represents a civilization to live in its own terms; or rather should one see this society as an instrument of production of goods in demand in western markets? If the latter, then this society has no importance, and is condemned.

Prices, in an economy in which contracts operate, must necessarily be artificial. They must be established in terms of the royalties of the American base locations or of the petroleum resources in such a way that the producer's remuneration at least equals that of a high-up office employee or of an engineer. In fact when one examines the fluctuation in production and consumption in these hunting societies one discovers that the key to production does not lie in some Eskimo psychodrama but rather in the politics of prices. And it is not in rerouting the native towards other activities without social support that opportunities to develop Eskimo societies will be released. Quite the contrary, the answer lies in allowing the Eskimo, at least where he wishes to do so, to exercise his traditional activities more profitably. If this is not done, disintegration will quickly do its worst.

'Too late,' a number of hunters at Thule told me in 1972. 'Today the young are always in greater conflict with the old and they have hardly any confidence in themselves. They don't know any more who they are, and some of them will probably have to leave the country in the future. But to do what? And the ones who leave will be the cleverest young people, the ones who did best at

Bird hunting with nets in summer is much enjoyed. They are eaten raw. The greatest delicacy are little auks. left to decompose in skins.

Skins hang out to dry
in the summer sun, the
only time of year when
the landscape is relieved
by a little greenery.

school. Our hunting economy, which derives its solidarity from the active contribution of every individual will be thrown out of balance and further impoverished. The school creams off the élite from among our young hunters. They become technicians and can only find jobs in the south, out of their own country. The others, the less intelligent ones, remain with us. At school they don't learn how to use the kayak – which is essential. They are boarders for several months on end, separated from their families and so they are not schooled in the daily practice of hunting with their fathers. When they are adults they can't earn a living by hunting. Can't the administrators understand that our society forms a whole, that it depends on the effort of every individual, and that the departure of two or three personalities among the young of every village can end with the collapse of the entire delicately balanced system which is our life?

'In fact only the dogs, which are our true pleasure, still encourage us by the need to feed them to hunt regularly. The hunt is what gives us our satisfaction as men. Don't they know, down there in the south, that we don't just live in order to produce, but also in order to be ourselves? Together, and according to our own ways.

'For the rest, if people aren't careful this very ancient society will, with its solidarity, disappear. What powers are placed in our direction are just sweeteners. The example of the American base, with its territorial prohibitions and frustrations, is just one proof of this. We, the Eskimo, are not proprietors of our land as we understand it. What will it be like when they discover oil under our ground? To whom will it belong? Which capitalist society will benefit from it?'

But an entirely novel scheme would reduce the white man's role to that of consultant. The native community councils would take the responsibility of managing and financing the hunting activities; what the hunters were paid would correspond more closely to their actual production. The good years would make up for the bad years and the hunters' earnings could be kept fairly constant. It would be like a pool of resources from which the hunters drew what they needed according to what they produced, not according to the white trader's fancy.

When a bad year fell upon the hunters and they brought in too little, the council would subsidise their earnings from the pool. Of course if the hunters continued to bring in too little, then the council would have to reassess how much the hunters should be paid. But this plan would always be able to meet their needs in time of hardship and a program of assistance could be initiated before, not after, the event.

There is no example of an alienated society – such as that of the Polar Eskimo – which will not put itself back to work as and when it is apparent that this is on its own account. The people begin to live again when they know that their initiative will bring rewards that are truly in their own interests.

Chewing on a piece of sealskin
– used for boot soles – makes
it pliable, but some women's
teeth are worn
down to the gums.

97

West Greenland Eskimo

Little trace of Norse shows in
the Eskimo blood of these old
Greenlanders of Jakobshavn,
even though Eric the Red's
colony lasted from 986 to 1500.

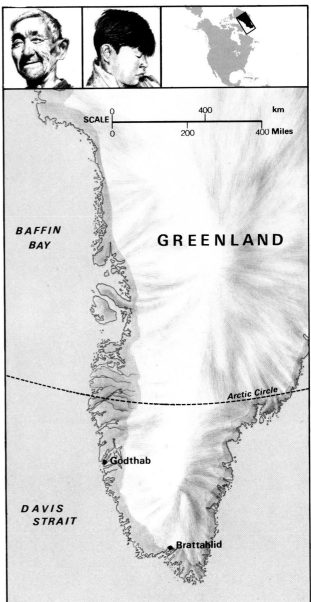

Erik the Red, the Norse adventurer, named this great island Greenland because of the color of its ice. As winter breaks, after weeks of false dawns that end the days of almost continuous night, a coast of broken mountains and glaciers is visible, and winter snow in a low sun. As summer mounts into days that rapidly lengthen into perpetual if steeply slanted sunlight, fragrant heather bursts out on the hard mountainsides, rock pools teem with unexpected insect life and stillness and peace spread over a sea strewn with icefloes. At the onset of winter the sky lies low and gray. The wind beats up from the wide open Davis Strait; the sea rolls heavily like molten lead.

In a cove behind a lonely skerry settlement, a handful 99

West Greenland Eskimo

Unmarried women wear white
thigh-length seal skin *mukluks*;
married women wear red,
widows black. Pants are made
of fur-appliquéd dog skin.

of turf huts are scattered among the ice-polished rocks. A short way across the water two kayaks approach the shore. They are dark specks in the swell, appearing then disappearing over the waves, slender craft with the grace of seals paddled by men clothed in glistening watertight skin smocks. Occasionally a wave washes over them, but none can find a way into the kayaks. The water-tight dress is laced tightly to the rim of the manhole in the craft and also round the wrists and face of the paddlers. The kayaks capsize with an easy motion, then are righted just as easily. The harpoons are held to the deck by stretched thongs, ready to be seized at the proper moment when the shape of a seal appears. Never still, the Eskimo seal hunters seem as one with their kayaks, as practised in the arts of hunting, as expert in the ways of the sea as their forefathers in Greenland many hundred of years before.

The history of the Eskimo in Greenland reaches back more than 4,000 years. In those times, when the climate in Greenland was considerably drier and milder than it is today, the first Eskimo crossed Smith Sound from Ellesmere Island to extend their hunting into the tundra of northern Greenland. The shores were less lofty then, which meant the island was much smaller in those remote years; the sea was undoubtedly less full of ice than it is in our day when in many parts ice-free waters are

Because the permafrost prevents
graves being dug, the dead at
Upernavik lie beneath cairns
of stone. Christian crosses are
a recent addition.

only a high-summer phenomenon. By way of this passage to northern Greenland Eskimo families, or family groups, seem to have traveled continuously. Some chose a north-eastern route when they ventured into the new land; others turned south. But for those who took the southern route there were innumerable hazards in the glaciers and the ice sheets which crossed their path. In west Greenland beyond Melville Bay there are few traces of Eskimo settlement from this period. The first flush of Eskimo settlement in these parts comes later, between 1400 and 500 BC, when the migrations to west Greenland brought people who possessed what is called a 'Bone and Stone Age culture'.

These Eskimo had a preference for promontories when they chose a site on which to build the houses with their low peat walls and skin roofs. Usually these houses were raised somewhat from the ground and placed at the foot of a cluster of rocks. Armed with bows and arrows, they hunted the reindeer from shooting stands raised like the houses above the beach. They hunted seals on the ice and fished by the shore or in the rivers. But it seems that these Eskimo died out some time between 700 and 500 BC, and for the following 600 or 800 years silence reigned along the coastlands of western Greenland. Then, with the migration of Eskimo from far in the west around Hudson Bay, the stillness was broken again by human speech, by the sound of the stone-cutter's hammer, by the tinkling of flint flakes split off the core with the flaking tool. Smoke from domestic fires of Eskimo settlements once again pricked the nostrils of wild animals in west Greenland.

There were many notable differences in the tools of these Eskimo who, at the earliest, arrived and spread south into west Greenland around 100 BC. On land they were ineffective hunters. They owned no bows and arrows, but instead used heavy hunting spears; fishing spears were barbed; blubber lamps were square unlike those of their predecessors; their houses also were built square and in later periods the floors were sunk beneath the ground. There is no doubt that the Eskimo of both these periods lived in much the same way: by a combination of land hunting and capturing sea mammals like the seal and the walrus. But according to the archaeological finds, the particular tools of this culture did not endure for long. In the first half of the 12th century, we encounter the first written testimony regarding these Eskimo – an account of Erik the Red's discovery of Greenland in AD 896 as recorded in Are Frode's *Islendingabok*. The narrative relates 'They there found, both towards east and west, traces of human dwellings as well as fragments of small boats made of skin and such instruments of stone which made it clear that the same kind of people had lived there who have peopled Vinland and whom the Greenlanders (i.e. Norsemen living in Greenland) called Skraelings.' From this evidence we may assume that the Eskimo had used skin boats, and yet by this time they

themselves had left the region of west Greenland. It was, it seems, a deserted land that met the eyes of the Norsemen.

We can only guess at the reasons for those Eskimo deserting west Greenland – it may even be that there were some still remaining even at the time the Norsemen arrived – but isolated clues give part of the picture. At around AD 500 a somewhat colder and more moist climate set in. At one place they stayed on until the 9th century, but generally it seems that they were unable to cope with the damp cold in their flimsy houses which were heated by open fires needing constant attention. Much fuel was also needed and quite possibly the lack of it was a prompting to decamp. When the immediate vicinity of the settlement had been exhausted of fuel, the task of gathering from remoter parts may have become too arduous. Driftwood may also have been exhausted; and the cold could not be warded off without fire.

Towards the end of the 12th century (less than 100 years after Are Frode wrote the *Islendingabok*) a new Eskimo culture had reached so far south in west Greenland that the Norse people could speak of Skraelings. A small work, *The History of Norway*, written around AD 1300 relates 'On the other side, towards the north of the

(Top) The midnight sun casts an eerie light over the brightly painted houses of Godthaab, Greenland's capital, founded by Norwegians in 1721.

People say that the old stone and turf homes, though smoky, were warmer than modern wood and tarpaper shacks where most Greenlanders live now.

Greenlanders (Norsemen) hunters have found some very small people whom they call Skraelings, and who when wounded alive by weapons die without loss of blood, but whose blood, when they are dead, will not cease flowing; but iron they lack entirely and use walrus tusks for arrow heads and pointed stones for knives.' These Eskimo were more sophisticated than their predecessors; they used the kayak, although this was a far less elegant maneuverable craft than the modern kayak.

They used sleds and dog-teams, bird darts, soapstone lamps and pots, spacious stone and peat houses in which whale ribs were used as rafters. It is possible that this culture originated in Siberia, crossed the Bering Strait to Alaska and then spread rapidly along the northern coastlands of Canada. There they found favorable conditions for whales had hitherto had the free and un-challenged run of the open waters. These Eskimo had come to stay and in time they claimed Greenland for themselves and for their descendants. This immigration was the first link in an unbroken chain of immigrations which continued until the 1860s.

In the *History of Norway* is the first mention of an en-counter between the early Norse settlers and the Eskimo. That this was not always a peaceful affair is made clear by the way in which the 'small men's' reaction to wounds is emphasized. As Norsemen traveled north along the coast of west Greenland they often encountered Eskimo dwellings and although the Icelandic Sagas are curiously reticent on the matter of Skraelings this by no means displays a lack of knowledge of them – it rather suggests that their presence was an everyday matter, and so to be avoided by a narrator of Sagas. Furthermore the Skrael-ings were not Christians but shamanists and members of the Catholic Church could not converse with them. Yet if a harmony existed between Norsemen and Eskimo at this time, it was not to last. About the middle of the 14th century the most northerly Norse settlement in west Greenland was destroyed by Eskimo. And although the final destruction of all the Norse settlements is shrouded in mystery, it would seem that this came about as the Eskimo migrated south during a time in which the climate was growing much colder and the herds of seals returned in profusion to the southern coasts of west Greenland. In 1578, when Sir Martin Frobisher landed in Greenland, he found no Norsemen, only Eskimo.

It is remarkable that European influence did not begin to leave its traces on the west Greenland Eskimo culture until after the middle of the 17th century. In the preceding years there had been many voyages to Greenland, and European sailors (from English, Danish, Dutch and Basque ships among others) brought back many accounts of the west Greenland Eskimo. In 1608 the Dane Lyschander tells us 'The average man is sturdy and strong, well built and with good limbs, but generally wan and pale . . . They (the women) wear many pairs of *hoser*, and in them conceal knife, needle and thread, and

other indispensable things . . . Their boats are long and slender and pointed, they use them as well and with the same mastery as a rider his horse. The boats are all sewn of gray seal skin, so stretched over an ingenious wooden frame, that a man can hardly be seated there. On top a hole has been made, which is so narrow you can scarcely get into it. To that you fix your coat by laces. With the hood on the head and the paddle in the hand, they think nothing of wind and water, but let the sea be repelled.'

During the 17th century the west Greenland culture developed along its own lines and according to the conditions which prevailed along the coasts; further-more, at this time, distinct geographical divisions began to emerge between the various Greenland cultures. North Greenland developed a Polar Eskimo character which marks it out from the others; similarly a north-east Greenland culture group developed quite distinct from that which was formed in the rest of east Greenland. For west Greenland Eskimo the two most important factors were the whaling industry, and the Europeans. As hunting in the open sea, in the ice-free sounds, in the fairways between the numerous islands and in the bays and fjords became more common, the Eskimo settle-ments gradually became more dispersed along the whole coast. Hunting from the ice grew less important, especially in the parts of west Greenland where only thin ice covered the water. Open water hunting – except hunting for whales which demanded a group effort in an umiak, a much larger craft than the kayak – became the domain of individuals in kayaks, and large numbers of small settlements were established. This also affected the houses, for until then they had usually been small and round. Then they became larger and more rectangular, sometimes housing several families. Inland the Eskimo still hunted reindeer and other animals, taking the sleds drawn by dog teams from the winter houses to the summer tents.

On the west coast of Greenland the influence of the Danish colonists, who first arrived during the 18th century, was more profound than elsewhere. Here the Europeans considered that the expenses of colonization could be readily covered by the proceeds of trade. The exports from west Greenland consisted largely of blubber and sealskins and in return the Eskimo received cereals, hard tack, rice, sugar, coffee and other foods, and Christianity. Almost as much as the new tools which Europeans brought with them, the new foods contributed to a change in the economy of the Eskimo. But of course the greatest revolution in their lives was the introduction of firearms which enabled the land hunters to dispense with bow and arrow and spear. Only at sea did the harpoon remain the primary weapon.

The great Eskimo hunters and heroes of legend were always early risers. The hunter steps outside to look at the sea or the ice. If there is a possibility of going hunting he makes everything ready, and with nothing but

It takes much courage and skill to go out after whale in such a small boat. The old hunters, though, used the small and frail skin-covered umiak.

Since the rich shrimp and prawn grounds were discovered off Greenland, canning and quick-freezing have become important industries.

The cold bleak sea which appears to provide nothing but ice gives the Greenlanders almost everything, from whales to tiny fish called *augmagset*.

a cup of very hot coffee he takes himself out for the day. In the meantime the women go to the trading store with their blubber or sealskins or down, and buy whatever they need – fishing hooks, twine, perhaps a knife or a pair of scissors, and tobacco. For the women the remainder of the day is spent in sewing or dressing the sealskins until, towards evening when they expect the men back, they begin to prepare the meal.

Early in the evening everyone retires to bed. But as long as the midnight sun eliminates notion of day and night these common practices are not strictly observed. Sundays, however, are strictly celebrated along with the other Christian festivals; but of the ancient, pagan Eskimo rites little remains among west Greenland Eskimo, except perhaps a single remnant on Twelfth Night when young people dress up and move about the scattered settlements in masks and occasionally with huge model phalli. Otherwise it is the arrival of guests, or the meeting with people from various dwellings that inspire feats and entertainments filled with music of a European fashion.

The daily life of these Eskimo has always been hard, though to some extent it is easier in these days, and the seal hunter who has spent his day locked in the kayak will return to his home to rest with a pipe of tobacco. Only on the hunting ground, when there comes a pause in the hunt, do the young men turn to sport and rivalry in games of strength or agility. They may wrestle, pull at hooks with arms or fingers, or even play football which their distant ancestors first played with crew of John Davis' ship in 1586. In all the west Greenland communities, now served with trading stores, churches, schools and even farms, the Eskimo have a great fondness for the children. The boys may play at hunters, throwing harpoons from their first kayaks which are no more than outlines of stones set on the beach. But as soon as the boy catches his first seal his childhood is at an end. Good or evil, life now lies before him.

Ammassalamiut
East Greenland

104

An Ammassalamiut kayak is just
big enough for the fisherman
and his equipment. Its frame
of driftwood from Siberia is
covered with stitched skins.

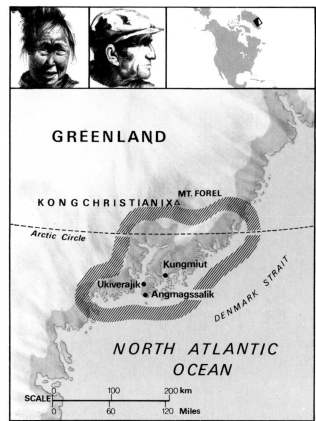

GREENLAND

KONG CHRISTIANIX△   MT. FOREL

Arctic Circle

Kungmiut

Ukiverajik●   ●Angmagssalik

DENMARK STRAIT

NORTH ATLANTIC OCEAN

SCALE
0	100	200 km
0	60	120 Miles

The Ammassalimiut, who are sometimes called the capelin people after a small fish of the salmon family, live strung out from the shores of Siberia along the Arctic coast of east Greenland in three great fjords between 65° and 67° latitude north. They are the most oriental of the Eskimo people and have lived here in isolation for centuries. To the east of them is a major obstacle to navigation, a great wall of ice 160 miles wide. To the west the continental ice-cap stretches 1,280 miles across. South and north of them the nearest settlements are 1,600 miles away. The Ammassalimiut's mongoloid ancestors came here in successive waves from Asia, across the Bering Strait. They were discovered in 1884 by a Dane, G Holm. He recorded that there were then 413 Ammassalimiut.

For two months the sun does not appear above the mountains. In winter, from mid-September to mid-May, the Ammassalimiut live in big patriarchal houses. All who are born in this house are first cousins and so may not intermarry. Some of the men, subject to the agreement of their first wife, have two wives.

The walls of the big patriarchal winter houses are made of clods of turf and flat stones. You enter its single rectangular room by a long, low doorless corridor, the only means of ventilation. Two windows of translucent seal intestine look out to the south-west. In temperatures 105

Ammassalamiut East Greenland

In summer, strips of cod dry
hanging on caribou antlers
stuck amongst arctic sedge,
the main caribou food. Carved
antlers are sold to tourists.

An Ammassalamiut house of turf
and stone slabs is one
rectangular room, lined and
partitioned with sealskin.
Windows are of seal-gut.

inside the house which average 18° by day and 10° by
night the children go naked and the adults wear nothing
but a leather g-string.

Across the back wall of the room is a vast stone-tiled
platform covered with skins, which is divided by sealskins into compartments. Here the men carve the bone
or ivory of the sea-unicorn. Before each married woman
is a soapstone lamp with a long horizontal wick of
lichen burning in seal fat.

The guardian of this flame, the unique source of light
and warmth, she prepares the food for the daily meal:
boiled seal's meat, blanched algae and raw fat with
melted snow-water to drink. Sometimes there will be
frozen seal's brains or liver, or dried intestine, or root
plants conserved in leather bottles. The wife prepares
the skins and the sinew threads and cuts and sews the fur
and leather clothing. She cuts up the game according
to the traditional method and distributes it according to
degrees of kinship. The hunter himself only gets a very
small portion of his game but will receive better morsels
from his brothers and brothers-in-law. The sealskins
go to the hunter's mother or, when she dies, to his wife.

In winter the men hunt on the ice-wall in four- to
eight-dog sleds. They lie in wait during the dark winter
by the breathing holes of the resident seals. If the prey is a
polar bear its skin and head belong to the first man who
spots it. Its body is divided between the first four to
catch it. The Ammassalimiut hunters attract sharks to
the surface of a hole in the ice with putrefied meat. The
animal's liver is toxic and is used to burn in lamps. Its
meat is but a famine food for men: after it has been
drained and dried it is fed to the dogs.

From May onwards when the ice-wall breaks up the
Eskimo hunt the migrant seals by kayak. Each of the
families splits up and by umiak and kayak they leave the
winter houses for the more numerous great pyramidal
tents covered with old umiak skins and lined with fur.
Then in June all come together again in the fjord where

106

As the traditional way of
life based on hunting has
disappeared, many east
Greenland villagers have become
dependent on welfare payments.

the capelin spawn. There they harpoon salmon at the mouth of torrents. And they gather great quantities of plants - angelica, sorrel and bilberries. A young Ammassalimiut couple, after a marriage by abduction, set up their household in the boy's father's house. When a child is born it is named after an ancestor who has recently died. The name of the ancestor reincarnated in the child brings with it the dead man's relations of kinship and also certain aspects of his destiny. Thus there are two kinship systems - of naming and of biology - by which links are established in this communal society. Should the 'name' be unhappy in his new abode he leaves it.

A dead man is dressed in his best clothes by his relations and rolled up in a skin. He is then either placed in a tiled tomb covered with stones or he is cast, with his weapons and his tools, into the sea. For three days his relatives cease all activities. They mourn in a house without fire, without pronouncing his name. They empty the house, wash themselves and take new clothes. The souls of dead men are feared until they take up residence in the body of a child.

The Ammassalimiut face their deaths with calm. Suicides, which they consider as ethical, unexceptionable acts of individual liberty, are common. Sick old people can commit suicide and ask for help in doing so. In times of want a widow may cast herself with her children into the water to avoid burdening her group.

Winter is the time when Ammassalimiut households pay each other visits. The hospitality is on a grand scale. Seals which have been frozen are eaten 'high'; a performer, who is sometimes masked, dances and sings comic sketches to a drum accompaniment. Men and women alike show, with great freedom of sexual expression, what marvellous story-tellers they are.

Sometimes two Ammassalimiut will temporarily swap wives. In doing so they establish a mutual bond of assistance. At the time of the winter visits, during the ceremony of turning off the lamps, sexual promiscuity sometimes develops. Then the only restriction is on relationships with any kin who are closer than fourth cousins. Men may kill themselves with a harpoon for a woman. But more frequently they will provoke a duel with a drum. Before spectators, who play the role of a court, each takes his turn to sing aggressive satirical poems directed against his adversary.

When there is trouble in the group, or somebody falls sick, the *angakok* (shaman) summons up the auxiliary spirits. In the winter house, with the lamps out, the *angakok* screws his hands tightly behind his back and journeys either towards the Man of the Moon, the custodian of observance of prohibitions, or the Woman of the Sea, mistress of the hunting animals, who has been mulitated and soiled by the sins of men. The metaphysical thought on which these rites are founded is highly elaborate. Some experts in magic create composite beings, or *tulipat*, from human or animal bones

with which to kill their enemies. These *tulipat* will, if they fail, recoil and turn against their creator.

Ammassalik has by its isolation been a conservation area. Here, for example, are conserved the sacred vocabulary of the *angakok* and the Ammassalimiut's own technique for hunting on the ice. But years after the Ammassalimiut were discovered in the last century a Lutheran mission and a trading post were set up. Around 1920 all the Ammassalimiut were baptized. The people's cultural heritage was destroyed.

The Danes controlled the Ammassalimiut's contacts with western techniques - guns, cloth, metal - ensuring that they were gradual and progressive. In 1935 Ammassalimiut hunting and food remained practically as it had always been. Then in 1941 the Americans disembarked. They brought with them a technical revolution.

The descendants of the first-discovered 413 are now 2,600. As child mortality fell, genetic disorders made their appearance. The standard of living grows. Hunter's sons are public employees. Dental decay, respiratory and venereal diseases have all appeared. In three generations the Ammassalimiut have simultaneously experienced a demographic explosion and the shipwreck of a culture.

People of Iceland

Iceland is supported by her
fishermen. Their jobs are hard.
To prevent the ship capsizing
they must hack her free from
the weight of ice on the rigging.

The Icelanders are the youngest nation in Europe. Their island is also the youngest land-mass. In this infinitely old world it is only 11 million years since Iceland began to emerge from the North Atlantic ocean in a series of titanic volcanic eruptions – in geological terms a mere blink of an eye compared with neighboring Greenland, which is 4,500 million years old. Similarly it is only 1,100 years since Iceland was first occupied by Viking adventurers, and a mere 30 years since it became an independent republic in 1944.

The name Iceland is distinctly misleading. Unlike Greenland it is by no means a 'land of ice'. Nor is it an Arctic country for it lies to the south of the Arctic circle. In the high hinterland there remain some formidable and wicked glaciers crouched on a brawling mass of mountains, the relics of the last Ice Age 10,000 years ago. But all round the coasts there are green and fertile valleys, once well wooded, but now given over to grazing-lands for sheep, cattle and ponies. The Arctic currents and winds from the north are tempered by a 109

People of Iceland

In 300 years Reykjavík has grown from a farming village to the modern capital of a new nation whose people have all the grit of their Viking ancestors.

Smoke and flames rise from the Öldugígar crater as if the ancient god Thor was at work deep in the earth with his hammer and anvil.

branch of the Gulf Stream which girdles the island with warmth. This century has seen an appreciable rise in the mean temperature, both summer and winter. Iceland is getting warmer all the time.

It is a much larger country than most people realize – almost as large as England, for instance. Conversely, the population is much smaller than people expect – only just over 200,000, no more than the population of a small European city. Of these, nearly half live in and around the capital, Reykjavík, in the south-west of the island. The rest live in townships and villages round the coast or on scattered farms in the coastal valleys.

Iceland is one of the five Nordic countries, both culturally and historically. It was settled by land-hungry Norsemen in the second half of the 9th century AD, when it was virgin and uninhabited. There is no evidence that any indigenous people had ever lived there before. The Norsemen came mainly from western Norway, either directly or via the Norse domains of Scotland and Ireland; and so there was a perceptible Celtic strain in the original composition of the people. Today, however, Iceland is a separate independent nation with a distinct identity, culture, and language of its own. This is due to three main factors – environment, isolation and a profound sense of history.

Iceland is the only European country that can remember its own beginnings. The very earliest Icelandic historians compiled accounts of the first settlers (about 400 of them) and their descendants while memories of the Settlement Age (AD 874–930) were still fresh in the mind. In the year 930 the leaders of the various communities that had sprung up came together to create a political commonwealth, with an annual general assembly, the *Althing*, for the whole nation. It met for two weeks every summer in a magnificent natural amphitheater of riven lava at Thingvellir (Parliament Plains), some 30 miles east of the present capital of Reykjavík. Here the nation's leaders debated and passed laws, juries passed verdicts on court cases, and the whole nation gathered in a hectic, colorful jamboree to meet and exchange trade-goods and gossip. The nation that was born at Thingvellir in the year 930 was a unique creation for the Middle Ages: not a monarchy but a republic, a democracy.

Ultimately it failed. The early Commonwealth lasted for little more than three centuries. In 1262 the Icelanders accepted the King of Norway as their own king. Iceland now became a Scandinavian colony, first of Norway and then of Denmark.

The centuries of colonial status – 1262 to 1944 – were Iceland's dark ages. Denmark stripped Iceland of political and commercial liberties. All trade had to be conducted through Denmark. Iceland managed to maintain some sort of contact with Europe, but the

111

Hot springs near Reykjavík provide central heating for the whole city as well as a warm playground for the children in mid-winter.

Iceland has no minerals or valuable natural resources but is surrounded by richly endowed coastal fisheries, the basis of her prosperity.

(Bottom) Young puffins which are taken from the hillside burrows where they are hatched, taste rather like fish when they are salted.

isolation was severe. It was compounded by a marked deterioration in the climate. In the 15th century a little ice age set in all over Europe. In Iceland, right at the edge of the habitable world (habitable for Europeans, that is to say), the effect was disastrous. Livestock froze to death. Famine stalked the land. Farmers and their starving families waited desperately for the spring that never came, or came too late. At the same time volcanic activity increased, and catastrophic eruptions would smother the pastures with a poisonous shroud of ash. By the end of the 18th century, when Iceland was at its lowest ebb, the population had been reduced to 30,000. The wonder is that anyone survived at all.

But the Icelanders did hang on, grimly and doggedly. And in the 19th century the tide at last began to turn. In Europe reform and revolution were in the air. In Iceland independence movements inspired by continuing memories of a past greatness sprang up, and the long battle to achieve political liberty again began. It culminated a hundred years later with the foundation of the republic in 1944. Once again, not a drop of blood was shed.

Iceland emerged from the long ordeal of the dark ages remarkably intact. Isolation had had one redeeming factor: the Icelandic language, untouched by foreign commercial and cultural influences, remained a pristine form of Norse while the rest of the Scandinavian languages were all modified and altered. The Icelanders could always read and understand their own classical literature, the Sagas, and continued to write poetry and prose in their own classical language. All round the country the Sagas were read aloud in the farmhouses every evening. Guttering lamps of codliver oil glowed feebly over the worn manuscripts in the hands of the reader as the rest of the household toiled at their evening tasks and drank in the stories of the past. Despite extremes of poverty and squalid housing conditions in turf-and-stone-built hovels, the Icelanders remained an intensely literate people.

Literature helped to retain the sense of national identity intact. So too did the environment. Iceland is still being created, geologically. It is nature's workship, still smoking and blazing in a fury of production, with a volcanic eruption on average once every five years. It gives the country a brash, disheveled look compared with the balding veterans of the older continents, still quick with the life that forged it in the bowels of the earth, cruelly tempered by the shock of ice. And yet – such is the paradox of human nature – the more terrible the tribulations, the more passionate the attachment of the Icelanders to their land.

Compared with other European countries, prosperity came late to Iceland. It had no coal or oil to fuel an industrial revolution, no rich timberlands to sell, and not much capital to invest in what natural resources there were – hydro-power, natural hot water, and above all the fish that teem in the surrounding seas on Iceland's

After long days of brutally hard work an Icelandic trawlerman heads for home with his hold full of codfish, before the approaching storm.

(Bottom) On board a modern whaler, literally a floating factory, men flense — strip off the blubber and skin — from their gigantic catch.

continental shelf. Recovery and development in the first half of the 20th century was painfully slow. But since World War II, since independence, it has been phenomenally fast.

Iceland, one might say, never had a 19th century at all. It jumped straight from the Middle Ages into the 20th century, straight from the pony to the airplane, bypassing the railway age altogether. There were no roads at all in Iceland until the beginning of this century and no wheeled traffic of any kind. There were no villages, just scattered farms and seasonal fishing stations. Three hundred years ago, Reykjavík was just a farm; today it is the miniature metropolis of the north.

The change is superficially most apparent in their housing. Traditionally the Icelanders used rubble, turf, and driftwood for building because timber was inordinately expensive to import, and volcanic stone little suited to building. After the war, cement production was started, and for the first time the Icelanders were able to build high as well as wide, using pre-stressed concrete to guard against the danger of earthquakes.

Similarly, the only fuel the Icelanders used to have was peat, sheep-droppings and scrubs. Although surrounded by boiling hot water, bubbling and gushing out of the ground they had neither the technological skill nor the capital to harness it. Now it is being harnessed. Practically the whole of the city of Reykjavík is centrally heated by water piped from natural hotsprings. And scientists have estimated that if all this natural energy were harnessed, Iceland could produce about 70 million giga-calories a year – the equivalent of seven million tons of oil, but at a price six times lower than oil. Cheap electricity, too, from rivers has enabled Iceland to set up an aluminium smelting plant.

But the basis of all Iceland's prosperity is fish. It is as if nature, having created a land without minerals, compensated by giving Iceland richly-endowed coastal fisheries on its continental shelf beneath the sea. Iceland may have to import all its luxuries and many of its necessities, but she can pay for them in fish and fish-products.

Paradoxically, the major problem facing Iceland is now not one of poverty but of affluence. This could be the greatest threat to its unique culture and civilization. The Icelanders could cope with adversity – but what about good fortune? It is my contention that there is little need for concern. Iceland has none of the flaws and fractures that cause disintegration under pressure, no smouldering resentments nourished by centuries of class discrimination, no social jealousies or caste. In the calamities of the past, as cosmic forces brawled about his ears, the Icelander trod a wary but never despairing path, ultimately secure in his faith in his own unique identity. He had come to terms with his past, for past and present were two concentric worlds and he inhabited them both with confidence and ease. The future holds no terrors for him.

Lapps
Norway, Sweden, Finland and USS

Reindeer-sled racing over the frozen river is a big attraction during the great Easter festival at Kautokeino in Norway before the spring migration.

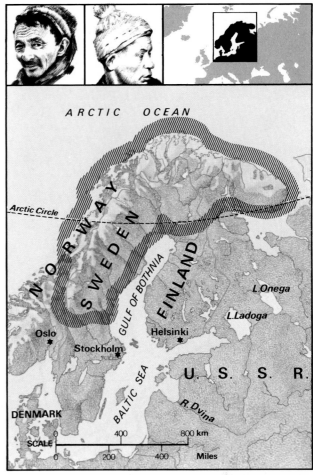

For the Lapp reindeer nomads, clustered in the wooden huts amid the endless snow which covers their land, winter is the quietest time of year. But the early spring is dramatic as the snow begins to melt and a crust of ice forms on the surface overnight. The trees are still thick with the whiteness, but soon slight breezes may shake the branches and the snow crumbles away in fine clouds. And little by little the crust of ice on the snow is thick enough to carry the reindeer. Then they begin an uneasy move towards the mountains where, in May, the does will calve. For the Lapp nomads everything must be prepared, everything gathered for the migration. The draft reindeer are tied to the sleds on which all the baggage, the food, tents and clothes, is packed. Ahead of them lies a journey of some 200 miles which must be covered in a matter of days. The herds must be watched day and night, kept together through fog or a snowstorm. Often the Lapps are in such a hurry that they cannot even afford to make regular night quarters. And then, if they do raise the tent coverings over the thin, conical frameworks, these may easily be blown away in the night.

115

During the migration the
Lapps sleep in a *lavo*, birch
poles covered with homemade
woolen blankets. Branches and
skins cover the tent floor.

As the day breaks men and women, and even the children, are hurried into activity. It is only the old who stay behind in the winter camp. For them the migration would be too demanding. They watch as the great herd of reindeer trickle across the snow and the Lapp nomads trudge behind with most of their worldly belongings piled upon sleds. Dogs race about at the heels of reindeer who have wandered off to graze. The whole camp moves slowly northward. For these nomadic Lapps the migration is as inevitable as the coming of spring. Their calendar is determined as much by the breeding and feeding habits of their animals as by the seasons.

In the northern parts of Norway, Sweden and Finland, which are often known as Lapland, and in the north-western parts of Russia, there are probably no more than 6,000 Lapps who still lead the life of reindeer nomads. The other Lapps who may number around 29,000 (there

are no recent census figures) make their living in a variety of ways, often completely removed from the near self-sufficiency of reindeer nomadism. Some make their living from the sea as fishermen. Others have turned to agriculture and a settled way of life, while there are many who work in the industries of northern Scandinavia or have drifted south to the cities. And yet the distinctive way of life of the reindeer nomads, which is so frequently associated with the Lapps, is not an ancient tradition and was never the way of all Lapps. Their culture and language (which is related to Finnish) is probably some 2,000 years old and even in the earliest times there were Lapps who led more settled lives around the coastlands. It seems that most, however, were hunters of the reindeer rather than breeders and herders. Only with the gradual northward movement of other Scandinavian people, and the depletion of the reindeer themselves, did

Children now have to attend
school in the village and
it is a rare treat for the
whole family to go on the
migration together.

some Lapps turn to breeding and herding the animals. The assimilation of the Lapps into the societies of northern Scandinavia is part of an old process. And the reindeer nomads are the Lapps who have resisted this process longest and most thoroughly. In the history of the Lapp people, other Scandinavians have always played an important part.

Even the very earliest descriptions of northern Europe mention the Lapps. And Lapland is indicated on some of the first maps of the region. In ancient times Lappish settlements covered most of Finland, Norway and Sweden, stretching from the White Sea to the Atlantic, and from the Baltic to the Arctic Ocean. Written sources as recent as the Middle Ages – reveal that the Lapps inhabited most of Finland, while at about the same time the Norwegian sagas indicate a more southerly settlement of Lapps in Norway and Sweden than at present.

These areas are largely the same today, except in Finland, where the southern limit of Lapp habitation has moved significantly northwards.

Much of the region is woodland, a country of marshlands and lakes. In the west, enormous wild and barren mountains rise in complex ranges which plunge into steep narrow valleys and fjords along the coast. Here the country is more varied than in other regions of the world on the same latitudes. The enormous belt of forest and tundra, which stretches across both northern Europe and North America, is here compressed into a narrow strip along the Atlantic coast. The sea, which brings warm currents from the south, creates a mild coastal climate and flora in the west which otherwise is only found in more southerly latitudes.

Until the middle of the 18th century this region was not divided by national boundaries. However, the then 117

Fishing and hunting are more
ancient Lapp occupations
than reindeer herding. Even
the herders sometimes fish
to supplement their diet.

Baltic coast and colonization continued inland up the broad valleys into Swedish Lapland. As late as 1100 AD, however, the Finns had not reached far north. But, during the next 600 years their slash-and-burn farming advanced rapidly northwards. By the mid 18th century they had displaced the Lapps as far north as the top of the Gulf of Bottnia. In the east it was not until the 16th century that Russian missions and monasteries were established in Lapland. Finally, in the last century, a small number of nomadic Komir and Samoyed migrated across to the Kola peninsula.

This was the approximate picture of Lapland and its peoples before industrialization, within a few decades, spread over the entire area. This recent process created a kind of settlement which is now dominant. Modern towns, with as many as 30,000 inhabitants, have sprung up both inland and along the coasts of Lapland. Large villages, mines, industries are now connected by roads and aircraft. But lonely farms and small hamlets may still be found along the fjords, on the high mountain plateaux, and in the desolate forest areas, where the way of life is still rooted in the old traditions.

equivalents of Russia, Sweden and Norway had for centuries asserted their interests through taxes, military fortifications and missionary work. The areas claimed by the various states were only defined by natural boundaries like mountain ranges, fjords and promontories. The watershed between Norway and Sweden was one of these features which was used as the initial basis for border negotiations and for final position of the frontier – eventually settled about 1750. However the frontier between Russia and Norway was not fixed until 1826, and that between Russia and Finland until 1919.

Archaeology reveals that the original inhabitants of this region were hunters and fishermen. In the earliest known descriptions these people are called *Finner* and *Skridfinner*. These are the names given by the ancient northern peoples to the Lapps. But in the meantime people living on the outskirts of the region were steadily penetrating deeper into Lapland. According to the first authentic account written about AD 900, settlements along the Atlantic coast reached approximately as far north as the present town of Tromsø. Some 400 years later a fortress and a church had both been built at Vardo, Norway's most easterly settlement. These new communities increasingly forced the Lapps further up the fjords as they spread inland.

118   The Swedes moved steadily northwards following the

After a long wait on top
of four or even six feet
of ice the fisherman's
patience is rewarded
with a lake trout.

The Lapps are a sea-faring
people like the Vikings.
Lapps were mentioned in an
ancient Nordic saga as
skilled boat builders.

The Lapps, who today number at most 35,000, are scattered over this vast area which has a total population of a couple of million. They live in every type of dwelling and with all kinds of occupations, singly, in groups, in villages or in larger areas where they still form the majority. In their lives, however, many are rapidly moving towards the routine of an industrial society. Only now, when it is almost too late, are intensive efforts being made to stem this process. The Lapp reindeer nomads are dying out, and yet through them it is still possible to sense the past and the traditional culture of the mountains, the tundra and snows of Lapland.

In these northerly regions, the original Lapp culture was not based on herding reindeer, but on hunting and trapping in the rivers and lakes, in the forests, on the barren plateaux and in the sea. Whales, seals, fish and seabirds were caught along the coasts; reindeer, moose, woodland birds and fresh water fish were caught inland. But as the Lapps came into increased contact with the advancing people from the south and east, trade began to play an ever more important part in their lives. In about AD 900 the Norwegian chieftain, Ottar, reported that the Lapps traded and paid their taxes with the furs of otter, bear and reindeer, with walrus and sealskin and with feathers and down. Later, however, ermine, squirrel and fox furs became equally important for the Lapps in their trade and for paying taxes. By the Middle Ages trade in Sweden and Finland was the monopoly of the merchants from Birkkala in Finland, and in Norway of the Bergen merchants. The enormous trade in skins and furs, which took place during these centuries, undoubtedly caused a serious reduction in the numbers of game and so undermined the very foundation of the Lapps' livelihood. It simultaneously fostered a new dependence on manufactured goods from elsewhere.

In particular, the trapping of wild reindeer both by individual Lapps and by groups was so intensive that the great wild herds were all but exterminated. The use of decoy animals is mentioned about AD 900. However, it has been reported that trapping by a series of pit-falls was also common at this time. The fences and corrals used in reindeer trapping in Siberia, Greenland and North America also occur in Lapland. Wild reindeer trapping must have been a cornerstone of Lapp livelihood. They hunted only in certain seasons, and these were generally followed by seasons fishing on the coast and along the inland rivers and lakes.

The Lapps divided their year into definite hunting seasons and migrated between relatively stable living quarters in the various hunting areas. The movements were also caused by the varying grazing pastures needed for tame reindeer kept by these Lapps both as decoy and as draft animals. The Lapps who spent the winters in the innermost parts of the fjords of Finnmark moved inland in the autumn, hunting wild reindeer and fishing the lakes and rivers; in the spring they again moved

Before the migration the herd must be inspected for fitness by government officials. Some bucks are also lassoed and castrated for sled deer.

(Bottom) This herd has to swim across to the summer pasture. The lead deer is coaxed into the water by the herdsman and then the rest will follow.

The herd moves to the coast
because their food, lichens and
moss, dry up in summer on the
inland pasture. Less flies
plague the coast as well.

121

(Over page) The great herd is
on the move. The Lapps have
no need to drive them, they
just follow the herd and guide
it to the family pasture.

A convoy of sleds, led by the
housewife, crosses the Finnmark
plain. She must look out for
stragglers – does calving early
or yearlings falling behind.

towards the coast. In the Finnish forests however, the
Lapps moved only between summer and winter quarters.
The so-called Skolt Lapps from the region south of
Varanger fjord continued this yearly cycle right up into
the 20th century.

In the 16th and 17th centuries, the herds of wild
reindeer diminished rapidly. But they were gradually
replaced by herds of tame reindeer bred from those
originally domesticated by the hunting Lapps. A whole
new way of life evolved – nomadism. Hunting Lapps
from the coasts, and from the inland regions, became
nomads. Reindeer breeding expanded rapidly over the
entire area, from the outermost coastal strip, over the
high mountain plateaux and through the vast forests. It
soon overran the old trapping and grazing territories of
the hunting Lapps. Reindeer nomadism developed in
different ways according to whether the Lapps lived in
the forests or in the mountains – and the different kinds
of nomadism are reflected in the length of the migratory
routes. The forest Lapps' reindeer herds had shorter
routes and used nearby high ground in winter and the

forests during the summer; the mountain herds migrated
annually up to 200 miles from the high mountain ranges
and the coast during summer, to the outskirts of the
forests for the winter.

For these Lapps the pastures and the herds provided
everything – from wood for the tents and fires, to skins
for their clothes. Only as trade with other people
increased, and a money economy took over, were the
skins and meat from the reindeer sold. This demanded
bigger herds, and far larger pastures. Today there are
vast herds ranging almost unchecked over enormous
areas; but they only support a small number of Lapps.
In Norway there are about 1,800 nomadic reindeer-
herding Lapps, in Sweden 3,000 and in Finland 1,500.

At about the same time as nomadism first developed
the coastal hunting and fishing Lapps were forced to
turn more and more to the sea as a source of their food.
Archaeological finds show that their hunting and
fishing traditions reach far back into Lapp history. Old
sagas describe the Lapps as famous boatbuilders and in
one, *Eigils Saga*, we are told that they built two Viking

Before the trek the wife lays out racks of meat to dry and bakes about 30 loaves of bread. The men carry bottles of 96 per cent home-brewed alcohol.

ships, which were sewn together with animal sinews. In the 17th century the Norwegian priest Petter Dass praised the Lapps' abilities as boatbuilders. Boats and fishing equipment were vital elements in their ancient coastal culture.

By the 16th and 17th centuries, however, Norwegian people were already firmly settled in coastal fishing villages, and the Lapps were introduced to the Norwegian culture by ever increasing trade. Here the cultural exchanges throughout the centuries wiped out almost all the differences between the two peoples. Nevertheless the sea Lapps have preserved many of their old traditions, like their houses, clothes and furniture, longer than the rest of the population. Until the turn of the century, most lived in turf cottages; cups and other utensils were made at home from knobs of wood, planks and wood strips. Their Lappish clothes were made of handwoven frieze cloth or seal, reindeer, sheep or goat skin.

Over the centuries stock farming had gained a foothold in the lives of the coastal Lapps and it gradually became characteristic. Lapps combined this with

The snow scooter has almost completely replaced the reindeer sled. One scooter costs 30 reindeer and rarely lasts more than 2 years – Lapps are hard drivers.

hunting and fishing. Cattle were driven to summer pastures and here the Lapps altered their settlements to cope with the buildings and techniques required for stock farming.

This was the pattern of life for coastal Lapps at the turn of the century when there came an explosive development in the fishing industry. The most dramatic changes were motors for the boats, and the building of decked – rather than open – boats. At the same time, the trend towards a monetary economy intensified. The coastal Lapps found it difficult to adjust their lives to all these changes and it was only after World War II that the development in their communities reached the general level. They achieved this mainly during the era of reconstruction which followed the devastation of the war. And now the villages of coastal Lapps have become so much a part of the general cultural scene that they are almost indistinguishable.

Inland, too, there were changes – especially to the semi-permanent living quarters. From ancient times the hunting Lapps had lived in small and scattered communities all of which had their own territories, usually along a watercourse or beside a lake. These Lapps made only short migrations between seasonal living quarters. For many people the depletion of game made these treks unnecessary, and one of the seasonal settlements was chosen as a permanent home. In many communities fishing in lakes and rivers became steadily more important while in parts the old migration pattern continued as well – as among the fishing Lapps around Lake Enare in Finland. Reindeer breeding was continued as the demand for meat and skins increased. But just as with the coastal Lapps stockfarming and agriculture finally played a larger and more important role in the economy of the inland Lapps. Where possible, fields were plowed and planted with grain and potatoes.

It has already been described how the other Scandinavians gradually pushed their way into Lapland. The Lapps offered little resistance to this outside pressure. As far as is known, they never took up arms against the newcomers. Negotiations and cunning have been their only defense, which is natural enough for a people who have always contended with the inexorable forces of nature. The traditional Lapp social system, which consisted of a large number of small local communities called *siidat*, scattered over the entire region and with no common organization, did not provide any platform for action. The basic element of each local community was the family, and the *siida* council was made up of the senior members of the families. Contact between neighboring *siidat* occurred only when they had common or conflicting interests.

As long as the Lapps' social system remained intact, the *siidat* were able to meet on behalf of their members. But in time the authority and influence of the *siidat* diminished. In the 17th and 18th centuries it was common

126

Easter is the Lapp time for reunions and weddings. Married in a Norwegian Lutheran church, the bride wears as much gold jewelry as she can.

for Norwegian, Swedish and Finnish officials to infiltrate the Lapps' societies by appointing as their representative the family chief most respected in the *siidat*.

In Finland infiltration was largely in the shape of widespread intermarriage between Finns and Lapps. In Sweden it occurred, especially in early times, through the taxation of the *siidat* districts and later by the allotment of these districts to new colonists. Territories which the Lapps had naturally regarded as their own were taken away from them.

The same thing was accomplished in Norway by designating the Lapps' territories as crown property, to be rented out, with the right to levy taxes for the national treasury. All these measures were serious encroachments into the fundamental elements of the Lapps' social system, and became important as causes of its internal disintegration.

Although their traditions could preserve some of the ancient social structure the Lapps were confronted with a new system at the very time when their own familiar society was collapsing. Their ancient ways and traditional culture were no longer able to support them and Lapps were forced to decide for themselves what attitude to adopt in the face of these cultural and social pressures. Individuals, without the cloak of a successful society around them, could only fall back onto their own

Many Lapps no longer spend the summer making reindeer butter and cheese as they used to. Instead they set up camp along the main tourist routes.

initiative and skills. It was in this milieu that the Lapp minority faced the rapid spread of industrialization over this region about the time of the World War II. The problems of the Lapps stood out in marked contrast to the progress of other Scandinavians and Finns towards a welfare state and an affluent society.

The difficulty of assessing their actual number reflects the attitude of many Lapps to these very problems. In places where there is no doubt which of the people are Lapps, their numbers are rapidly increasing. But in many other places it is impossible to collect any accurate material. This is especially true of coastal regions of Norway, where only a fraction of the predominantly Lapp population acknowledges itself as Lapp.

The pressures to which Lapps have been subjected by the other peoples of Scandinavia, Finland and Russia and by the deliberate minority policies of their governments, have been responsible for this attitude. Where Lapps have lived side by side with other peoples in a Lapp environment all have lived on equal terms. But where the Lapp communities have been isolated, the majority peoples have looked down on the Lapps. In the past the governments of Lapland made great efforts to erase much of the Lapp culture. But more recently the trend has been reversed and more positive moves have been made towards both integrating the Lapps and preserving much of the culture and language. A number of Lapp organizations have been founded, now under the umbrella of the Northern Lapp Council, which seek to preserve the cultural heritage of their people. This pro-Lapp outlook is not a romantic wish, but a desire to rescue many Lapps from a social degradation and assist them in developing a better way of life. 127

(Top) Lapps were originally shamanists and old superstitions linger, but they follow Russian and Scandinavian faiths now.

Lapps lie buried in the Russian Orthodox cemetery at Sevettijärvi in Finland. In the old days a bag of their belongings was put in the grave.

Chukchi
USSR

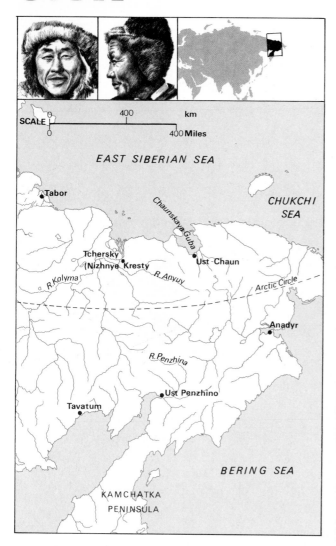

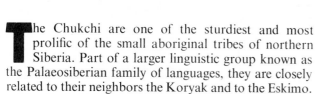

The Chukchi are one of the sturdiest and most prolific of the small aboriginal tribes of northern Siberia. Part of a larger linguistic group known as the Palaeosiberian family of languages, they are closely related to their neighbors the Koryak and to the Eskimo.

The Chukchi divide into two subgroups. There are the Reindeer Chukchi who are the greatest reindeer breeders in the world, and the Maritime Chukchi, who live by fishing and by hunting sea mammals, especially the seal and the whale. Only the Reindeer Chukchi, who are by far the larger group, should be called Chukchi for Chukchi means 'rich in reindeer'. The Maritime Chukchi call themselves Anqualit, 'sea people'. The two groups together distinguish themselves from other tribes by calling themselves Luoravetlans, 'the real people'. This is their official name among the Soviets.

There are now altogether about 12,000 Chukchi. Their
128 territory which stretches from the Anadyr river in

Chukchi are born into their
furs and live in them all
their lives. Small and hardy,
they were the last tribe
to submit to Russian rule.

'Chukchi' means 'rich in
reindeer'. The deerherds
mean food, transportation,
clothing, shelter, leather
and bone for tools.

Chukotka in the east as far as the tundra between the
Arctic ocean and the left bank of the Lower Kolyma in
the west, must be one of the most inhospitable of all
the inhabited regions of the world. Under the tsar
and under Stalin it was the site of the harshest and most
dreaded of forced labor camps: the area was officially
described as 'unfit for human habitation'.

Certainly the climate is very severe. A great deal of a
Chukchi's life is taken up with the problems of cold and
snow. When I, the first free westerner to go there for
50 years, began my visit to the land of the Chukchi, it
was early June. The worst of the winter was over. But
at Nizhnye Kresty (now renamed Tchersky), the tiny
capital of the vast Kolyma region, a bitter wind was
blowing off the east Siberian sea. After eight months of
winter ocean-going cargo ships, caught by a premature
freeze-up of the Kolyma river in September, were still
firmly held in the grip of the ice.

Not many years ago the annual break-up of the river
ice was a matter of life and death to the Chukchi communities who lived along its banks. In those days, having
survived the winter on stocks of frozen fish, by March
they had often used up their stores and they had to eat
the food they gave to their dogs. 'Everywhere' wrote an
eye-witness 'one saw famine-swollen, livid faces, with
fever-bright eyes from which despair looked out.'

All that has changed. Today the Chukchi are supplied
with all they need by ship during the brief summer and
by air during the long winter. They are no longer subject
to the vagaries of the seasons, to famine, disease and
intolerable hardships. Under the Soviet administration
their material circumstances have undergone immense
improvement. At the same time, however, their
indigenous culture has been systematically eroded and
to some extent russianized. The Chukchi are now, as a
tribal entity, at a transitional stage between a traditional
way of life and a new way of life worked out by Soviet
planners – with all the usual apparatus of state farms,
National Districts and centralized Party rule.

On first encounter, however, the Chukchi life-style
seemed unchanged. I had left Nizhnye Kresty by
helicopter and flown for several hours across the tundra
of Kolyma – a vast and featureless landscape of snow-
covered moss and sodden hummock grass – before a
herd of several thousand reindeer indicated the where-
abouts of one of the itinerant herdsmen's camps. We
touched down beside a huddle of traditional reindeer-
skin *yaranga* and stared out at a group of tiny, furry
figures clad from head to toe in skins.

Later, while a snowstorm swirled about the double-
walled tent that was to be our home in the tundra, the
Chukchi entertained us. An old woman brought in a

A sporting Chukchi shows off his skill and agility in lassoing a reindeer. His admiring young son. will soon take after him.

saucepan of boiled reindeer meat specially slaughtered in our honor. Exposed to a lifetime of wind and frost she had been worn away like a piece of driftwood on the beach. Her skin was as dry and cracked as ancient parchment and the northern climate had tanned it to a deep ruddy brown. This was the chief herdsman's mother. She was so old that no-one could guess the year of her birth or how many winters had passed since she had first traveled the bleak wastes of her homeland. She was, they confided in me, the last of the shamans of the tribe, the last of the exponents of the old life that had survived two hundred years of Russian rule and more than a generation of Soviet indoctrination.

The Chukchi, not surprisingly, were the last of the minority tribes of Asia to submit to Russian rule. Alone among the aboriginals of northern Siberia they effectively resisted the Russian pioneers who came to subdue and exploit them. Clad in old Japanese armor they fell upon the Cossack bands and Russian colonists with spears and lances and stolen flintlocks. Not until 1789, 150 years after most of the neighboring tribes, did they begin to pay a nominal tribute to the 'poor white chief' – the Tsar – and well into the 20th century some remained independent of Russian control. But the Russians had brought with them to Siberia three terrible weapons – smallpox, syphilis and vodka – against which the Chukchi had no defense. Epidemics of smallpox carried off hundreds at a time. Whole camps rotted with tertiary syphilis. The survivors would sell precious furs and the winter's fish store for a small keg of trader's

131

A handsome Chukchi is one with a head 'like a round grassy hummock', a moustache, and the ability to devour food as fast and noisily as a wolf.

Chukchi USSR

The Chukchi *yaranga* is very
similar to the tent of other
Siberian reindeer tribes:
a double layer of skins
covering a wooden frame.

When the tribe moves on the *yaranga* are left behind. New ones are fairly easy to assemble so there is no need to overload the reindeer.

(Center) The more settled coastal Chukchi live in huts along the coast. Many huts do not survive the winter and have to be rebuilt in spring.

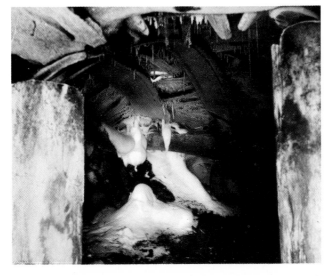

vodka. When they had drunk it they would sit down and weep with grief and frustration.

But the old life went on. With the spring thaw the Maritime Chukchi left their squalid permanent settlements along the coast to hunt the great beasts of the northern ocean in flimsy skin boats. Then the Reindeer Chukchi set out from their winter quarters at the edge of the forest where there was more shelter from the blizzards and better winter grazing for the herds, and started on their great circling migration across the tundra towards their summer pastures near the sea. To the Chukchi the reindeer meant transport, meat, clothing, shelter and leather and bone for their tools all in one.

Life was hard, virtually primeval. When they ran out of their staple food of meat or fish they would devour the bark of trees, catch field rats, or extract undigested vegetation from the intestines of reindeer. Even in good times their diet was by our standards revolting – raw frozen meat or old putrid meat, fermented blood, entrails, reindeer fly larvae, the contents of a walrus' bladder and bilberries boiled in deer fat. They had a form of dried smoked meat as hard and as tasteless as wood, and their main provision on long journeys was a large frozen meat ball. But of bread and most vegetables they knew nothing and they were obliged to do without salt. For drink they chewed frozen snow or a decoction of bilberries when they couldn't get tea. They chewed the dangerous fly agaric mushroom as an intoxicant and smoked suede leather when they couldn't obtain tobacco. They were ignorant of money and soap. They washed in their own urine and ate their own lice.

Short, stocky and immensely hardy, the Chukchi man and woman have an astonishing indifference to cold and fatigue and lack of sleep. Small children who have wriggled half-way out of their fur combination suits (fitted with moss diapers) can remain exposed to the winter weather without ill effect. In a temperature of

The Chukchi say: 'A finger in a ring is not a bolt on the door'; in the intimacy of the tent extra-marital relations are very common.

In summer the coastal Chukchi go to sea to hunt seal and walrus. Walrus tusks are gathered and made into various tools and implements.

Chukchi USSR

Chukchi wrestle not only for sport and fun but to settle feuds. A man must pin the other's shoulders to the ground to be declared the winner.

Old photographs show Chukchi making fire the traditional way, by rubbing two bones together. Matches were among the things introduced by the Russians.

−30° women perspire so much over such a simple activity as sewing that they have to stuff snowballs down their bosoms to keep cool. In an exposed region without fuel for fire they can sleep in the open and walk for two weeks in damp clothes without catching a chill.

The Chukchi of Asia are closely related to the Eskimo of America. They have bronze complexions, light-colored skin, straight eyes, straight black hair, flat skulls, low foreheads, well-shaped noses, small hands and feet. A beautiful woman is one with some pubic hair, a large pelvis and a full figure. A handsome man is one with a head 'like a round grassy hummock', a moustache, and an ability to devour food as speedily and noisily as a wolf – truly heroic eaters could eat a whole reindeer at a sitting in the old days. They are very sensual people, erotic in gesture and obscene in language. Virgins are a rarity after puberty and adulterers are legion. In the heat and intimacy of the communal inner tent extra-marital relations of one sort or another are common. 'Married is not sold for slavery' they say. 'A finger in a ring is not a bolt on the door'.

The Chukchi are an obstinate and tenacious people, quick to anger (blood feuds once used to be frequent), but compassionate to people and animals in need, and fond of children. They are musical and like a fine voice and a good song. They are also eloquent in speech and their language is rich in poetic imagery and vivid metaphor. At one time – and probably still – their folklore was full of incantations to bring good luck and

In summer Chukchi country comes alive. Free of the ice, man and reindeer can enjoy the bog cotton blossom and the bright sunny nights.

protection against harm. The following incantation, to protect a new-born child, was performed over a small stone wrapped in leather and is a beautiful example of the innately poetic cast of Chukchi thought:

> You are not on this earth, you are within this stone. No wind may reach you; no iceberg may crush you, for it will break in pieces against the edge of the stone. You are not on this earth. In the open ocean there dwells a great sea-animal, born when the earth and the world were born. This animal is a sea-lion. Its back is like an island, covered with earth and stones. You are on its back.

Until fairly recently the camps of the Reindeer Chukchi were based on mutually interdependent family units. But not even the family was a stable institution. There was no word for family and the nearest term was *rayirin*, which means 'household'. If a person left the house he was no longer a member of the family. Monogamy was the usual form of marriage, but polygamy was common and divorce frequent. Group marriage, and the so-called 'prostitution of hospitality' was also rife.

As for religion, their view of the universe and the spirit world was complex indeed. In the days of their primitive prime they were animists:

> All that exists lives. The lamps walk around. The walls of the houses have voices of their own. Even the chamber-pot has a separate land and a separate voice. The skins sleeping in the bags talk at night. The antlers lying on the tombs arise at night and walk in procession around the mounds while the dead get up and visit the living.

There were thus innumerable spirits in the Chukchi scheme of things. Some, called *vairgit* – sun, moon, winds, or spirits of tents and houses – were benevolent. Then there were the evil spirits called *kelet:* one-eyed little horrors with an unhealthy passion for human livers; the 'monsters', including the killer whale and the mammoths (or their frozen remains); and the souls which lived inside people, animals and plants and which often assumed the form of a beetle and hummed like a bee. To travel from one world to the other these spirits could either enter through a hole under the pole star or take a step down in the direction of the dawn. Dead Chukchi inhabited the Aurora Borealis.

Much of this intricate corpus of pagan belief has vanished now, along with the shaman, or medicine man (or woman) who was the tribal repository of such beliefs and the mediator (by means of the techniques of trance and ecstasy) between the spirits and the people. Among the Chukchi shamanism was characterized by sex-changes in the personalities of the shamans, who thereafter contracted homosexual marriages. Even in tsarist times the Russian administration disapproved of shamanism and the Soviet authorities made great efforts to stamp it out. Among the Chukchi today it is for the most part no more than a curious memory.

In shamanist days Chukchi believed that the antlers on the tombs arose at night and walked around the mounds and that the dead visited the living.

Soviet authorities made great efforts to stamp out shamanism; few old shamans, like this one, relieving a man's pain with a magic stick, remain.

The new deal for the Chukchi was ordained less than two weeks after the 1917 Revolution and was contained in the Declaration of Rights of the Peoples of Russia. The first Commissar of Nationalities was Stalin, who had himself done time in a Kolyma penal settlement. The Committee of the North finally turned its attention to the Chukchi in 1928. The Soviet program was two-fold. It aimed first to restore national self-respect among the Chukchi, and second to provide them with a satisfactory material existence. Philologists prepared grammars of their language and invented an alphabet (later changed to the Russian cyrillic script). A literacy program was started and any aboriginal with literary gifts was published by the local Chukchi press or broadcast on the local Chukchi radio station (and more recently the local TV station). Poets emerged hot-foot from the ice age: the Chukchi writer, Rytkheu, is well known in the Soviet Union. At the Institute for Northern Peoples and the Northern Faculty of the University of Leningrad a small band of soviet-trained, ideologically acceptable ex-reindeer herdsmen trickled back to their homeland as doctors, teachers and scientists.

Between 1929 and 1933 both the Reindeer and Maritime Chukchi underwent the painful process of collectivization. This provoked bitter opposition and caused disastrous losses among the reindeer herds. But by the mid 1930s they began to reap the lavish Soviet aid program's benefits – modern hunting and fishing equipment, veterinary services, and the resettlement (still incomplete) of nomads into more permanent villages with schools, clinics, co-operative stores, bathhouses and training centers.

Today the Chukchi are the great reindeer herders of the Arctic and reindeer herding has become one of the most profitable forms of animal husbandry in the USSR. Reindeer meat is a vital source of protein in an otherwise hungry region. Soviet experts reckon that the north can carry up to 4.5 million head of domestic reindeer providing 100,000 tons of meat each year. Already there are over 2.5 million head. A whole new science has been built around the reindeer industry, and the reindeer's traditional enemies – wolves, bott flies, warble flies, hoof rot and anthrax – are now under control. Before long the northern peoples as well as the Russian immigrant populations of the new towns may be self-sufficient in meat, with a little left over for export to Japan.

Today the Chukchi reindeer herdsman is earning rather more, in cash and kind, than a factory worker in the south. Since he has less to spend his money on, the formerly impoverished aboriginal is becoming one of the new rich of the Siberian outback.

Such material prosperity, some critics say, has been achieved at a price. The Chukchi are outnumbered by Russians in their own territory and the real decisions in the administration of their tribe are made in Moscow. Their attitude to this situation is ambivalent. On the one hand they are grateful for what has been done. On the other they are frightened they will eventually lose their national identity. They may be healthy and wealthy but they have not increased in numbers. In 1897 census their population numbered 11,800. In the 1959 census it numbered 11,680. Nizhnye Kresty (or Tchersky) was a collection of wooden huts when I was there. Today it is a white man's town of 10,000 Russians living in big concrete apartments blocks who run an administrative center for a goldbearing region the size of Holland and Denmark together, earn the highest wages and eat the best food anywhere in the USSR.

In my tent in the Kolyma tundra day merged into night and back into day without visible distinction. I breakfasted on reindeer and brandy at three in the morning. It snowed and it rained and it thawed. The Chukchi came and went on sleds. The reindeer suckled their young calves. Every few days the herds moved on. The route of their migration, the clothes, the tents and sleds of the herdsmen had not changed in hundreds, perhaps thousands, of years. How much had their minds changed, their tribal pysche, their very being?

(Right) Chukchi are fond of children and keep them warm in fur combination suits. The younger ones have moss diapers to keep them dry.

Glossary

THE isolation of the Arctic regions has enabled the two major groups of native peoples, the Eskimo and the Indians, to remain unusually homogeneous. Both originated among the mongoloid peoples of central Asia. The Indians crossed to the American continent, about 30,000 years ago, long before the Eskimo, and spread south. The Eskimo settled throughout the Arctic but never ventured south of the tree-line.

There are over 80,000 Eskimo in the Arctic today and they are one of the most uniform peoples known, in physical type, language and culture. They are of medium height, powerfully built with straight noses and straight black hair. They are closely related to the Aleut, who have a similar culture, and to the other Siberian mongoloid people, the Chukchi.

The Indians of Alaska and Canada, who share the same mongoloid ancestry as the Eskimo, differ in appearance. Their faces are less flat, their noses are more prominent and they have slightly darker skins.

The Lapps are small and dark-haired. They are a Finno-Ugrian people whose ancestors came from the Ural region and spread through Scandinavia.

All of the Arctic peoples have adapted physically in various ways to the harsh climate. The mongoloid people have accumulated fatty deposits on the parts of their bodies that are habitually exposed to the cold – cheeks, eyelids, hands and feet. The Lapps, who are small and slender, have adapted in a different way. The veins on their arms and legs lie close together so that heat can circulate easily and quickly from the warm outgoing arterial blood to the cool incoming venous blood.

The material culture of all the Arctic peoples is basically the same from Norway to Greenland. Inland, caribou or reindeer are herded or hunted together with small fur-bearing animals. Coastal peoples are fishermen and hunters whose most important prey are the large sea-mammals.

There have been many separate migrations and explorations of the Arctic by northern European peoples. These began with the Celts and Norsemen who discovered Newfoundland and settled Iceland and Greenland. Russian Cossack adventurers spread through Siberia, the Aleutian Islands and North America as far south as California in search of furs. Adventurers flocked to Alaska and Canada in their thousands during the 19th century in search of gold. But it is only in the last 30 years that the Arctic has become one of the greatest development areas in the world.

The realization, on both sides of the narrow Bering Strait, of the strategic importance of the region and of its potentially vast mineral deposits have turned the Arctic into a booming frontier land,

---

AIVILIK *see* **SOUTHAMPTON ISLAND ESKIMO**

ALEUT *Population:* 1,000. Language group: Eskimauan. Most of the remaining Aleut live in the United States' part of the Aleutian Islands off Alaska, though some 400 live in the USSR islands of Medney and Bering. The Aleut were once avid hunters of seals, beaver and fox furs. They used seal-skin kayaks to hunt seals, or cross the heavy seas between the islands. Until the 1780s, when the Russo-American company forced all male Aleut to hunt furs for them, the Aleut were divided into warring clans, led by elders, which sometimes took slaves. Despite the years of exploitation that were to follow, certain benefits, like the introduction of cattle and pigs, were brought to the islands. Today the islanders' fur trade is based less on fur-hunting than on fur-farming – and many hunters now make their living fishing, or as small-scale farmers.

ANGMAGSALIK *Population:* 300. Language group: Eskimauan. The Angmagsalik Eskimo live in the east of Greenland; fishing, hunting and trapping are their principal means of survival. Their hunting bands were based on kin groups and their marriages entailed little ritual except giving a few gifts to the bride. The women practised a form of birth control by refraining from sexual relations for two years after the birth of a child. Men competed with each other in contests of physical skill. The women worked leather, gathered wild vegetables and fruit and helped build the huts and boats. Angmagsalik lived in semi-underground huts built of stone with gabled turf roofs and sometimes in semicircular skin tents. When a man died his eldest son inherited most of his movable property. Land, however, was owned by the community.

ATTAWAPISKAT *Population:* unknown. Language group: Algonkian. The Attawapiskat led a semi-nomadic life just south-west of Hudson Bay in Canada. They lived chiefly by hunting sea-animals like seals, fishing and collecting wild vegetables and fruits. Collecting these wild foods was the work of Attawapiskat women. Families who were interrelated lived in small clusters, led by a headman. Before a man married – preferably his mother's brother's daughter or his father's sister's daughter – he worked for his bride's parents. Contests were often held to test men's strength and skill. Women worked leather and men made boats, but both built the half-underground circular turf huts or bark tents in which they lived. Sons inherited their father's property equally.

BAFFINLAND ESKIMO (see pages 62–85)

BEAVER *Population:* 400. Language group: Northern Athapaskan. The Beaver are semi-nomadic Indians who live chiefly by gathering, hunting and fishing near the Hay and Peace rivers south-west of Canada's Caribou Mountains. The women dress skins and work leather, gather wild foods, make the circular thatched huts and help build the boats. Men spend most of their time hunting. Girls are married off very young to avoid premarital pregnancy, usually to a young man from the same area. On his marriage a man presents gifts to his bride and sets up house with her near her parents. When a man dies his property is either destroyed or given away.

CANADIANS *Population:* 22 million. Languages: English and French. Canada, the second largest country in the world, has a relatively small population, especially in the far north where the stretches of desolate country are broken by a population of 2 people or less per square mile. The racial origins of the Canadians are related to the country's historical development. The original Indians and Eskimo, though now increasing, numbered only 200,000 in 1961. At the same time the French-Canadians numbered some 5 million, descendants of British settlers about 9 million and of other Europeans about 7 million. In the frozen

north, snow-bound and isolated for much of the year, there are still one or two descendants of the old settlers, gold miners and trappers who came to these parts to make their fortune or escape the strictures of city life. These people – most only part or temporarily employed still rely heavily on fishing, trapping and hunting for their livelihood. In Labrador in particular there is little other employment, and few schools or roads. Canada is a small self-governing, independent nation, the oldest and largest of the British Dominions which stretches across the larger part of the North American continent. The national culture is based on two languages, English and French, and on the varying racial and religious traditions of its inhabitants.

CARIBOU ESKIMO (see pages 62–85)

CHUGACH *Population:* 200. Language group: Eskimauan. These Eskimo lived in the Chugach Islands and nearby coast of south-western Alaska in settled villages. Fish and seals provided the major part of the diet – supplemented by a little gathering of wild foods and hunting local animals. The Chugach married after a token gift had been made to the bride. The couple would then normally live close by the man's parents. A man could not marry either his father's brother's daughter or his mother's sister's daughter. Premarital sex, although forbidden, was common among young people. Rules which prohibited intercourse for several months after childbirth, however, were strictly observed. Adolescent boys had a hut to themselves and did not sleep with their families. Some Chugach, hereditary 'aristocrats', once kept slaves, but now only control land. When a man died his property was divided between his sons, who received equal shares, and his daughters who received less. The Chugach lived in wooden huts, with flat bark or gabled wooden roofs.

CHUKCHI (see pages 128–137)

COPPER ESKIMO (see pages 62–85)

DOGRIB *Population:* 900. Language group: Northern Athapaskan. The Dogrib are a

semi-nomadic tribe of Indians who live east of the Great Slave Lake in Canada. They once lived only by gathering, hunting and fishing and were led in all activities by informally elected headmen. Women made the small boats and leather, gathered wild foods and helped in the fishing. The men, who did all the hunting, made the conical skin tents which have now been replaced by gabled log houses. A marriage was marked by gifts to the bride and couples either lived on their own or with the man's family.

DOLGAN *Population:* 1,500. Language group: Yakut. The Dolgan live mostly in the Taymyr National Okrug in northern USSR. They fell under the influence of the Russians in the 18th century and until the Revolution had to pay high fur taxes. Nomadic reindeer herders and fishermen, the Dolgan also hunted the polar fox, wild reindeer and various birds with bows and arrows. They sometimes used decoy reindeer for hunting and held collective hunts at water crossings. Their arrows, and later their bullets, were poisoned with rancid reindeer fat. They fished in summer from dugout canoes. Once they lived mainly in tents and fixed huts but later dwelt in huts on sleds. The Dolgan were socially organized around the clan. As the fur trade developed collective ownership of property gave way to individual ownership – which eventually led to great inequalities in wealth. The Dolgan were once unusual for their matriarchies in which groups of families elected women to rule the men. The women also organized their worship. Today the reindeer herds are owned by collectives, fur-hunting is organized on a large scale and the Dolgan live in houses instead of the skin tents and huts.

ENTSI *Population:* 500. Language group: Samoyedic. The Entsi live around the Yenisey, Little Kheta and Pur rivers, and Lake Pyasino in northern Siberia. In the past they lived by hunting reindeer, polar fox and by fishing. Some reindeer were bred as pack animals and unless a man owned a large herd, he would not kill his own stock. The Entsi organized themselves into clans, and clan members could not marry each other. Their wealth was very unevenly distributed. Rich leaders would own up to 3,000 head of reindeer, while the poorer majority often had no more than one or two. Today the Entsi run a major fishing industry using modern fishing boats. The fur trade has been developed – especially polar fox. Reindeer are hunted with high-powered rifles instead of with traps and spears and the people are no longer nomadic. Only fishermen and hunters do not live all the year round in the settlements where schools are now provided for the children.

EVEN *Population:* 12,000. Language group: Tunguso-Manchurian. The Even live in the land between the east Siberian and Chukchi Seas and the Bering and Okhotsk Seas. All Even have had frequent contact with other peoples like the Evenki (q.v.) and the Yukagir (q.v.) and are at least bilingual. While most were traditionally nomadic reindeer breeders and hunters, some lived settled lives along the coast fishing and hunting, where they used dogs rather than reindeer for transport. Squirrel and seal hunting were always important activities for them. Nomadic Even built birchbark tents or houses with carefully prepared and tied bundles of sticks. Clans were the basis of their social organization. Each clan was led by elected elders. There were great differences in wealth between the rich reindeer owners and the poorer hunters and herders. Today the reindeer are owned and herded collectively and farming, fur hunting and fishing have all been developed on a large scale.

EVENKI *Population:* 25,000. Language group: Tunguso-Manchurian. The Evenki live in the area west of Okhotsk coast and Sakhalin and north of the Upper Tunguska, Amur and Lake Baikal in USSR. (Some Evenki also live in China and Mongolia.) The northern and southern Evenki in the USSR are often considered as different groups. In the north they hunt and breed reindeer. In the south they breed cattle and horses and even cultivate the land. Under the Tsars they were heavily taxed. To represent the very large clans, the Evenki used to elect a 'prince' who was held responsible to the tsar for a period of three years. The Evenki hunter's equipment once included a decoy reindeer, special rucksacks and sleds. Rich Evenki never hunted but bred their animals or paid others to do so. Sometimes skins were drenched in water, frozen into the shape of a trough and then used as a sled. Reindeer were used for

transport and their milk, meat and skins were all put to use. Some people were skilled blacksmiths. Tents were often made by women out of birchbark, but the kind of house differed according to the wealth and occupation of the individual. Social organization was based on membership of a clan with hunting as a frequent collective undertaking. The Evenki became Orthodox Christians, but continued to be greatly influenced by their own magical beliefs, rituals and shamans. Today they are well educated and although industry is as yet hardly developed, hunting, fishing, trapping and reindeer breeding provide a good income.

EYAK *Population:* 50. Language group: Eyak. The Eyak live in settled villages around Prince William sound, Alaska. Fishing, hunting and gathering are their major sources of food. Each person belongs to one of two major clans. A man may not marry the daughter of either his father's brother or his mother's sister. In the past adolescent boys did not live with their parents but went to live with relatives elsewhere until they married. Women worked leather and gathered wild fruits; men hunted, fished and built log cabins and boats. Socially there are distinct rich and poor people and in the past some Eyak kept slaves. Eyak headmen are succeeded by the son of a brother or sister, and property is inherited in the same way.

GREENLANDERS *Population:* 35,000. Language groups: Scandinavian and Eskimauan. The earliest settlers are thought to be Eskimo who arrived in Greenland from North America about 4,000 years ago. Norsemen, who came by way of Iceland, arrived about 1,000 AD, and some went to discover America – which they called Vinland. In 1261 Greenland recognized the king of Norway as its sovereign, mainly to secure supplies for the country. But communications between the two lands were slowly neglected. Eskimo from the north of Greenland attacked and destroyed Norse settlements – by the 15th century communications with Norway had ceased – and by about 1500 the Norse people became all but extinct. New settlements from Europe did not get under way again until the 18th century. Today most native Greenlanders are of mixed Eskimo-Danish origin. Some Eskimo, however, live in igloos, turf or wooden

huts, fishing and hunting for a living. Other Greenlanders operate a large fishing industry, sheep farms or one of a few other industries. In 1933 the whole of Greenland was declared a dependency of Denmark (which before had sovereignty only over eastern Greenland) and today Greenlanders have seats in the Danish parliament. **(see Polar Eskimo pages 86–97, West Greenland Eskimo pages 98–103, East Greenland Eskimo pages 104–107.)**

ICELANDERS *Population:* 19,000. Language group: Scandinavian. The Icelanders are descendants of Norsemen and their Irish slaves and monks who first colonized the island about 1,200 years ago. Today they still speak an almost pure form of Old Norse. Most people live around the coast and about half in Reykjavik the capital. Despite its name, Iceland is still actively volcanic. The people tap the hot, volcanic springs for hot water, central heating and even greenhouses in which they grow tropical fruits like bananas. Icelanders tend to be socially egalitarian, a tradition dating back to the earliest settlers who regarded 'all free men as equal'. Fishermen may earn as much as professors and there are no social titles. The country also has the world's oldest parliament, founded in 930 AD. Fish and fish products (mainly cod, haddock and herring) account for 95 per cent of the country's exports. There is no army and the standard of living is among the highest in the world. A shortage of labor means that people often work 60 hours a week, sometimes in two or three jobs. A rapid increase in population, despite much emigration to America in the late 19th century, followed a rising standard of living along with a low divorce rate. There is also a high rate of illegitimacy (some 27 per cent of births) and no social stigma is attached to the offspring. **(see pages 108–113)**

IGLOOLIK (see pages 62–85)

ITEL'MEN *Population:* 1,000. Language group: Paleoasiatic. Almost all the Itel'men have now merged with the Russians in the southern part of the Tigil'skiy Bayon in the Koryak National Okrug USSR. They were mainly salmon fishermen living along the banks of rivers in settled villages, who used both nettle-fiber nets and hooks. They also hunted seals and beavers. The Itel'men ate many different plants of the lily species which they gathered wild. Their huts were built half underground. Their villages consisted of the members of one clan, which would often feud with other clans. When they married husbands moved into their wives' huts and women often ruled the households. Fights over women were frequent as they were greatly desired as slaves. Their religion centered round a raven who was seen as the creator of all things and there were many other rituals associated with animals important to the economy. When adults died they were fed to the dogs; children were buried in hollow trees. After coming under Russian rule, the Itel'men rebelled repeatedly against oppression and taxation. The Russians have introduced horses, cattle and wheeled transport into their way of life. Today the Itel'men live in fishing collectives or on farms. Many more, however, now lead a life that is far removed from the ways of their fathers. Educated and conversant with technology, these Itel'men are almost completely russianized.

KASKA *Population:* 300. Language group: Northern Athapaskan. Most of the Kaska Indians now live integrated in Canadian society. But there are some who still lead semi-nomadic lives in the Cassiar Mountains in western Canada – gathering, hunting, trapping and fishing for their livelihood. Women play a large part in the life of the settlements, working leather, gathering wild foods and helping with the fishing. In the past before he married a man worked for his bride's parents, his bride being, for preference, the daughter of his mother's brother. Kaska settlements were made up of 50 or so relatives, mostly linked through the female line, living in round, turf buildings or gabled and thatched-roof huts. All social organization was based on clan membership. Sons inherited the property of their father equally, except that a daughter's husband would inherit the trapping lines.

KORYAK (see pages 130–135)

KOYUKON *Population:* unknown. Language group: Northern Athapaskan. The Koyukon Indians who live mainly in the drainage area of the Koyukuk river in Alaska used to trade with the Nunamiut (q.v.) and now the extinct Kobuk Eskimo. They are one of the most northerly Indian tribes. They lived by trapping and hunting in the forests of the area and used canoes, made of birchbark to move from place to place. They caught salmon in large numbers from the rivers and hunted river otters with bows and arrows. Their religion was controlled by shamans. Although they had warlike neighbors, the Kutchin (q.v.), the Koyukon hardly ever entered into war.

KUTCHIN *Population:* 350. Language group: Northern Athapaskan. There were once many populous Kutchin (or Tatht) tribes but nearly all are now extinct. A semi-nomadic branch of Kutchin lived near the Peel river in Canada's Yukon and North-Western Territories gathering wild fruits, fishing, trapping and hunting for their livelihood. They lived in skin tents or semi-underground wooden huts roofed with turf. Men sometimes married several wives, the marriage requiring only a few gifts to the bride, who could not be a first cousin of the groom. All Kutchin belonged to a clan with an ancestor as its head. Women worked leather and helped fish and built canoes. Although there are no social classes, some Kutchin are clearly richer than others. A mild form of slavery once existed, although slave status was not inherited. In the past chiefs were succeeded by their eldest sons who also inherited their property. Girls were permitted to have sexual relations with the young men before they married, but were punished if they became pregnant.

LABRADOR ESKIMO *Population:* over 1,000. Language group: Eskimauan. The Labrador Eskimo led a semi-nomadic life along the Labrador coast. They hunted deer, trapped, fished and hunted the seals and walruses along the coast. Men sometimes took more than one wife, giving various goods at the marriage ceremony to the girl's parents. Women worked leather and made a little pottery. Today these Eskimo are famed for their soapstone carvings. Bands of Labrador Eskimo were, in the past, led by hereditary headmen; at the time of death, as for all these Eskimo, a headman's property was either destroyed or given away. Sexual relations were once freely permitted, but with the coming of missionaries gradually became prohibited, at least officially. Their traditional igloos have now been replaced by timber buildings clustered together in small villages.

LAPPS (see pages 114–127)

MACKENZIE ESKIMO *Population:* unknown. Language group: Eskimauan. These Eskimo include several minor groups and are collectively called Mackenzie Eskimo only because they live in the Mackenzie delta region of north-west Canada. They trap, fish, hunt whales and seals and many small land animals. They used to travel by sleds and dog teams, or by kayak. Most of the Eskimo in this region were converted to Christianity at the beginning of the 20th century and this led to a marked change in their way of life. Their houses, for example, are now mostly built of timber. In the past these Eskimo were great

141

traders in tobacco, skins, knives and even iron pots which they brought over the ice to North America from Siberia. They are well known for their fine soapstone carvings.

MONTAGNAIS *Population:* 700. Language group: Algonkian. The Montagnais Indians now live mostly around Lake St John in Quebec. In the past they lived a semi-nomadic life gathering, fishing and hunting, though a few more settled villages had up to 2,000 inhabitants. Before marriage, preferably to his mother's brother's daughter, a man had to work first for his bride's parents. The girl was strictly required to be a virgin on marriage. The Montagnais lived in large family groups, and a man might sometimes take two wives. The women made leather, gathered wild fruits and vegetables, and helped build canoes and erect the bark or skin tents. Chiefs were succeeded by their eldest sons who also inherited their fathers' property.

NABESNA *Population:* 150. Language group: Northern Athapaskan. The Nabesna are a semi-nomadic tribe who lived by gathering, fishing and hunting between the White and Tanana rivers in Yukon and Alaska. Women worked at dressing the skins of small animals, and helping to raise the skin or bark huts. Hunting bands were led by headmen, chosen for their experience, age and ability. Before he married – customarily the daughter of his father's sister or of his mother's brother – a man had either to work for his bride's parents or make a token payment. Girls were married at puberty to avoid any possibility of premarital pregnancy. Men could have several wives in the past, but now have only one, and build their huts close to that of the bride's family. Men belong not to the clan of their father, but to the same clan as their mother and her brothers.

NAPASKIAK *Population:* 180. Language group: Eskimauan. The Napaskiak Eskimo live by the Kuskokwim river in Alaska and center round Napaskiak village (see pages 18–37). Most families have their own winter home solidly constructed of wood. They catch salmon and smelt in the river and salt them down before storing them for the winter months. They are also hunters, trapping mink for the fur trade during the autumn when separate camps are

established many miles away. During winter the men return to the village and then in the spring go back to the camps to hunt musk rats. In the spring sealing is very important. The people do not gather many wild foods. Marriages, which follow a period of great sexual freedom, are arranged by parents. The religion today is nominally a form of Russian Orthodoxy (brought by Russian missionaries many years ago), influenced by a number of traditional taboos and beliefs.

NETSILIK (see pages 48–61)

NGANASAN *Population:* 1,000. Language group: Samoyedic. The Nganasan are the northernmost people in the USSR and live in the Taymyr National Okrug. Reindeer hunting, instead of breeding, was their main traditional activity and their staple foods included reindeer, fish and duck. Hunting often involved whole communities. Clans formed the basis of most of their social organization: clan members, for instance, were forbidden to marry each other. A camp tended to center around a rich man who sometimes bred a great herd of reindeer, rather than hunting the animals. Men who could afford the bride-price had several wives. Their religion was based on the animistic belief that everything has a spirit. Sleds, for example, were told where they were going. Shamans possessed much influence. Everyone believed in life after death and in reincarnation. In winter the dead were not buried but left on sleds in the ice. Their only well-developed handicraft was leather working. The Russian Revolution touched the Nganasan very late, and only now is collective reindeer herding superseding hunting. They now also trap for

the fur trade. In recent years stores selling Russian goods and schools have also contributed to the changes brought upon the Nganasan by the Russians.

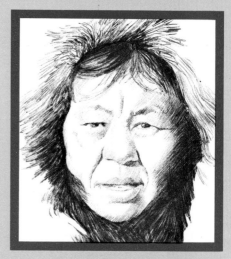

NUNAMIUT *Population:* 150. Language group: Eskimauan. The Nunamiut live in the central Brooks range of Alaska. They trap, fish and hunt caribou and other animals. In summer they gathered into large bands and lived in moss huts, hunting the herds of migrating caribou and the flocks of migrating birds. In winter they clustered in the turf huts of their villages and fished or hunted seals. Girls were normally married at puberty, and a marriage was signified only by the exchange of a few gifts and the formal consent of the parents. The man came to live close by his wife's family, for whom he also worked. It was not permitted for cousins to marry and although wives used to be freely exchanged, this too often led to jealousy and murder. Despite missionary efforts to influence them, they still hold many beliefs in spirits, and practise many non-Christian rituals.

NUNIVAK *Population:* unknown. Language group: Eskimauan. The Nunivak Eskimo live on Nunivak Island off the western coast of Alaska in wooden, turf-roofed, semi-underground houses. Traditionally they fished and hunted seals and whales, gathered wild fruits and vegetables and hunted small land animals. Women worked leather, made pots, gathered wild foods, helped build the huts and fish. Among the Nunivak there was no restriction on marrying a cousin and the couple normally lived near the man's family. At puberty boys were partially segregated from their families and had to sleep away from other members of their family. When a man died his eldest son inherited most of the property.

OSTYAK see SEL'KUP

POINT HOPE ESKIMO *Population:* 270. Language group: Eskimauan. These Eskimo have been settled at Point Hope, Alaska for over a century. Mainly through the influence of missionaries and teachers modern ways have become mixed with their traditional way of life. Today their houses are built of timber, but some still resemble their traditional semi-underground huts. They live by fishing from outboard motor-powered skin boats, and by hunting caribou and birds as well as whales and seals, which they store in underground caches. They are predominantly Christian, though they still observe some of their older beliefs, concerned with feasts for success in whale hunting. The summer months are the most difficult in which to gain a livelihood. Many of the men then leave their villages to find work elsewhere. For the first few years of their marriages couples live with relatives. Divorce is virtually non-existent.

POLAR ESKIMO (see pages 86–97)

RUSSIAN ESKIMO see YUGYT

RUSSIANS *Population:* 15 million. Language group: mostly Slavic. The Russians in these northern regions of the USSR originate from many different parts of Russia. The first were Russian Cossacks who conquered much of the area for the tsars in the 17th century and after, imposing taxes on the local tribes, but also settling down and intermarrying. Other groups of Russians became assimilated into the Cossack culture and became totally indistinguishable from the original Cossacks. Still other peoples drifted north, as traders and trappers then settled as farmers, while more are the descendants of exiles to the Siberian labor-camps and

mines. Today the life style of the northern Russians varies greatly – from reindeer herders to industrial laborers and engineers.

SAGDLIRMIUT see SOUTHAMPTON ISLAND ESKIMO

SEL'KUP *Population:* 6,000. Language group: Samoyedic. The homelands of the Sel'kup cover a vast region of northern Siberia, most of them living by the Tym and Ket rivers. Some 1,500 live north of the Arctic circle and in the Tay and Turukhan basins. The Sel'kup have long been subordinate to the Russians and from the 17th to early 20th century were forced to pay them high fur taxes. Only the most northern people bred reindeer. The rest lived by hunting and fishing and, at one time, by breeding foxes for their furs. They use dugout canoes in the summer months. The Sel'kup have totemic clans each of which is associated with a particular animal. The Bear Clan, for example, believes it is descended from a bear. Their houses are normally built on the river banks; in the north mud-covered wooden huts are common. In the past and only in summer did they live in birchbark tents. Most hunting and fishing expeditions are organized on a collective basis, and traditionally the people have been bound to help each other. Their religion is noted for its elaborate ritual which involves instruments used by the shamans – especially the tambourine, on which a shaman was believed secretly to fly. In more recent times agriculture and fur-farming have been developed. Towns have sprung up. Every village now has a school. And most of the people are literate.

SIVOKAKMEIT *Population:* 300. Language group: Eskimauan. These people live on Alaska's St Laurence Island in the Bering Sea. They fish and hunt seals, walruses and whales and trap and hunt land animals. Reindeer, introduced for breeding at the beginning of the century, had all died by 1950. In the past, the permanent settlements often held about 200 people. They once used to live in skin tents, but today their houses are made of wood with thatched roofs. Each village was divided into different sections for different clans.

Today the women dress the skins of small animals and seals caught by the men. Though they once also made pots, these are now imported from the mainland. A man normally marries his cousin, and before they can set up home together near his family, he must work for his bride's parents.

SLAVE *Population:* 400. Language group: Northern Athapaskan. The Slave Indians led semi-nomadic lives between Trout lake and the Great Slave lake in the North-west Territories of Canada. They built wooden huts with either conical or gabled roofs, clustered in small settlements of 50 to 100 people. They hunted, fished and gathered wild fruits and vegetables. Before marriage, a man had first to work for his bride's parents. Men often married several sisters. After their marriage the couple lived in the village of the man's parents. While the men hunted animals like squirrels, foxes and beavers, the women prepared the skins for trade and gathered all the wild foods essential to their diet.

SOUTHAMPTON ISLAND ESKIMO *Population:* 2,500. Language group: Eskimauan. The original Eskimo inhabitants of Southampton Island, north of Hudson Bay, were called the Sagdlirmiut. Although Europeans knew of their existence for many years, they only made real contact with them in the 1860s when whaling first began on a large scale in the area. In 1902 the last Sagdlirmiut were completely wiped out by typhoid. Soon Aivilik Eskimo from the mainland arrived to replace them. Then in 1924 the Hudson Bay Company arranged for more Eskimo to settle there to trap the furs needed by the company. All these Eskimo now live around Coral harbor. They hunt seals, polar bears, caribou, walruses, whales and foxes, and are notable for never having used skin boats, once so common among other Eskimo. They also fish and buy a variety of southern goods from the trading store. Less than 50 Europeans live on the island.

TAKAMIUT *Population:* 400. Language group: Eskimauan. The semi-nomadic Takamiut (or Taqagmuit) Eskimo lived in northern Labrador mostly by hunting large sea animals like seals, walruses and whales. They also fished through the ice, and hunted

143

and trapped on land. Marriage involved little formality except giving gifts to the bride. A man sometimes had two or more wives. It was customary for a man to marry his second cousin and although it was forbidden to marry a first cousin, he would occasionally do so. Today the people live either in igloos or more frequently in timber-built huts in large villages through the long winter. During the summer months they move into tents nearer their traps.

TANAINA *Population:* 650. Language group: Northern Athapaskan. The Tanaina Indians live in small settlements between the Chuguch and Wrangell Mountains in southern Alaska where they used to hunt, fish in the streams, trap and gather wild forest foods. Their houses were square, semi-underground wooden huts with gabled bark roofs. In their traditional way of life, everyone belonged to one of two clans. At puberty boys had to leave their parents and live with other relatives. When a girl was married it was considered essential for her to be a virgin. If she was not she would be severely punished for bringing dishonor on her family. The women did all the gathering of wild foods and leather work. There was a hereditary social class of men who controlled much of the land. Chiefs were always succeeded by a son.

TAQAGMIUT see TAKAMIUT

TATHT see KUTCHIN

TAVENMIUT *Population:* 1,000. Language group: Eskimauan. Until the beginning of the 20th century the Tavenmiut Eskimo lived chiefly along the north coast of Alaska. They found their food by hunting and trapping on land in the summer months and by fishing and hunting seals, walruses and whales throughout most of the year. Their houses were dome-shaped and made of turf or simply skin tents. A marriage demanded only a few token gifts to the bride. Some men could afford two or more wives, and newly wed couples generally lived near one or other of their parents. Settlements with over 100 people are mostly permanent, though some still remain semi-nomadic

moving out to trapping camps at certain times of the year. Today some of these Eskimo live in towns like Barrow.

TLINGIT *Population:* 5,000. Language group: Tlingit. The Tlingit Indians live in large settled villages by hunting, trapping and fishing in the islands and coastal strip of southwest Alaska. It was customary for a man to marry the daughter of his father's sister. Children belonged to the same clan as their mother. At puberty boys were forbidden to live with their parents and went to live with one of their mother's brothers. They became heirs both to their uncles' property and to their rank. Tlingit houses were large and held about 30 people. There were many ranks for the men, ranging from house leader to supreme chief. The Tlingit were famed for their 'potlatches', often held when a man died and his heir succeeded to his office. On these occasions different and sometimes hostile groups congregated together and held contests in dancing, feasting, singing and eating. Vast quantities of goods were destroyed or given away to enhance the prestige of the person who disposed of them.

YUGYT *Population:* 1,500. Language group: Eskimauan. The Eskimo in the USSR live along the north-eastern coastline round the Chukchi peninsula, from the Bering Strait to Kresta Bay and also on Vangel Island. The earliest Eskimo here lived in half-underground huts, but then developed tents and turf huts. Hunting seals, walruses and whales were always the major subsistence activities of these people. When American whalers reduced the numbers of whales, where before several Eskimo families had lived off one whale for a year many families now faced starvation. As trade with the Russians developed, tea-drinking became firmly established as part of the Eskimo culture and diet. Their traditional kayaks were slowly replaced by Russian-made boats. Former communal houses in which several families lived together were replaced by the late 19th century by wooden houses. Traditional tattooing of the face remained commonplace until recently. The main social unit once consisted of a rich man and a group of his relatives. As private property ownership developed with trade this unit broke down and the gap between rich and poor increased. The Eskimo religion centered around various spirits – often of

animals. Rituals entailed much dancing and through special rites the people hoped to protect and increase the whales and other animals. Both women and men could become shamans. Today many industries have been developed; whaling and sea fishing, manufacturing waterproof clothes from gut and skins, and collective reindeer breeding. Also the old skills like weaving, bone carving and the dressing of furs are encouraged by the state.

YUKAGIR *Population:* 1,000. Language group: Paleoasiatic. The Yukagir, who live along tributaries of the Kolyma river and the lower forests of the Kolyma and Alayeya have seen many changes in fortune throughout their history. In the 17th century they controlled vast areas of land with many subservient tribes and by all accounts lived well. In the early 19th century, however, this position was totally reversed. By the start of the 20th century Russian officials reported that the Yukagir were poverty-stricken and starving. Their numbers had been reduced by many thousands to fewer than 500. Today their numbers are still small, but both their two major collectives are prosperous. The Yukagir are now reindeer breeders and hunters. In the past, at the places where wild reindeer cross rivers, the people once made massive communal killings. They fished, hunted birds and other animals for their fur. During winter the Yukagir lived in huts; in summer they lived in tents. The catch from a hunt used to be distributed among all the members of a settlement, the skins going to those who killed the animals. When a man was married he went to live with his bride's parents, although in fact the couple were permitted sexual freedom long before their marriage. In all religious matters the people were led by shamans who, on their death, were cut up and their pieces kept as sacred relics. The Yukagir are noted for their writing. Early in their history they evolved a type of writing using pictures and symbols. Women tended to keep their writing for love letters, but men used it mostly to leave messages for hunting parties, together with maps and directions as to where game might be found. Today all Yukagir are settled with fishing, reindeer-breeding and fur-hunting all contributing to their regained prosperity.

(All population figures are approximate)